KOMMOS

Kommos

A Minoan Harbor Town and Greek Sanctuary in Southern Crete

Joseph W. Shaw

The American School of Classical Studies at Athens gratefully acknowledges the support of Jane Bracken. Without her generosity, the production of this book in color would not have been possible.

© Copyright 2006 The American School of Classical Studies at Athens
All rights reserved.

Originally published 2006 by The American School of Classical Studies at Athens
First published in Greece 2006 by Mystis

Book design by Mary Jane Gavenda, Publications Management

ISBN 960-6655-00-8

MYSTIS
15 Kalisperidon str., 713 07 Iraklio, Crete
Tel: +302810 226518 Fax: +302810 221908

Printed in Italy

For Maria

TABLE OF CONTENTS

FOREWORD — 9

CHRONOLOGICAL CHARTS — 11

PART I. THE KOMMOS SITE — 15
The Minoan Town
The Southern Area and the Monumental Minoan Buildings
The Greek Sanctuary (Southern Area)
Kommos and the Sea

PART II. PITSIDIA AND THE WESTERN MESARA — 61
The Pitsidia/Matala Community
The Western Mesara
"A Great Minoan Triangle"

PART III. THIRTY YEARS OF DIGGING — 83
Aims and Methods
Financing
The Beginning of a Dig: Some Personal Background
Negotiations
The First Days

PART IV. SOME THOUGHTS ON CONTRIBUTION   113
"The Strange and Wonderful"
"Minoan Palaces"
Two Monumental Stoas
The "Shipsheds"
Late Minoan II: "Independence at Last"
"Domestic Economy"
A Question of Attribution: Greek Temple C
The Artemis Temple in the Plain
Cretan Temples Updated—The "Dreros" Type
The "Phoenician" Shrine and Recognition
"Wrapping Up": A Conclusion

APPENDIX: THE WRITTEN WORD
AND THE DIGITAL DAWN   144
FURTHER READING   150
BIBLIOGRAPHY   152
CREDITS   162
INDEX   163

FOREWORD

An approach by Charles Watkinson of the American School of Classical Studies at Athens (ASCSA) about writing a short book such as this may have been due to rumors that I was already writing one. Although that was not true, I had considered one for some time. So, during my morning hours on Crete in 2004 writing up finds from House X for a final Kommos monograph, I gave the ASCSA offer consideration. It appealed to me. While we have written dozens of reports and numerous volumes about the Kommos site, their so-called Scientific Approach filters out humanistic aspects, the anxieties and difficulties, the excitement of discoveries, the beauty of a changing landscape in our small area in south-central Crete. Much of the poetry is lost. Although our excavation and personal diaries could fill a volume many times the size of this one, I thought a short description of the excavated area coupled with objectives, hopes, methods, and discoveries might be appealing.

For the many plans, elevations, and restorations I am indebted to our excavation architect, Giuliana Bianco, who also allowed me to choose several of her pen and ink sketches of local Pitsidian life. Taylor Dabney took many of the object photographs. I am also indebted to Mary Markou, who typed my manuscript and helped process the illustrations, and to Charles Watkinson and Timothy Wardell of the ASCSA for their much valued editorial assistance.

For other aspects of the work involved I thank the Social Sciences and Humanities Research Council of Canada, the Institute for Aegean Prehistory, the University of Toronto, and Lorne Wickerson. We thank the members of the Greek Antiquities Service for standing by us and for their help over the years.

The book is dedicated to my wife, Maria C. Shaw, for being a vital part of the Kommos project from its inception, for her insights, and for her role as assistant director and, along with others, in helping see the project through and to its publication. Accompanying us from the first day as excavation started in 1976 were our then infant children, son Alexander and daughter Robin, for whom Kommos and Pitsidia became a second home.

The book has also been written to give the people of Pitsidia a sense of the history of the site—of their own local history. We are indebted to them and hope they will be the spiritual wardens of the Kommos site and its shoreline. At the time of writing, consolidation of the scarps and ancient walls is being completed in preparation for its being opened to the public by the authorities. A plan suggesting paths, shelters, and viewing platforms has been submitted by us, and is under discussion. Occasionally visitors wishing to enter the site have, by prior arrangement, been taken to it by guards from Phaistos.

Joseph Shaw
Pitsidia, Crete
July 1, 2005

Chart 1. Chronology of Minoan and Greek Kommos

For the post-Neolithic, "Minoan" period, we use the system proposed by Arthur Evans. He divided the period into three phases (Early, Middle, Late Minoan) with numerical subdivisions (e.g., Late Minoan III [LM III]) that can be further subdivided (e.g., LM IIIA1). The sub-periods correspond roughly with changing ceramic form and decoration that can often be linked to architectural changes on sites. We occasionally refer to the times of the emergence of the Minoan palaces (MM IB–MM II) and their renewal (from MM III–LM I) as Protopalatial and Neopalatial, respectively.

3500–2000 B.C. Late Neolithic–Early Minoan Periods. At Kommos, only sparse occupation.

2000–1700 B.C. Middle Minoan IA–II Periods. The Kommos town spreads. The first large civic building (AA) is founded and later destroyed, perhaps by earthquake, at the end of MM IIB.

1700–1425 B.C. Middle Minoan III–Late Minoan I Periods. "Neopalatial Period." Kommos town expands. Building T is constructed at the beginning of the period, but gradually falls into disuse while life continues in the town.

1425–1375 B.C. Late Minoan II–IIIA1 Periods. Continued occupation. Destruction of Knossos in northern Crete at end of period.

1375–1200 B.C. Late Minoan IIIA2–IIIB Periods. A regional Mesara revival in LM IIIA2 brings about the construction of massive Building P, later abandoned along with the town.

1200–1020 B.C. Late Minoan IIIC–Subminoan Periods. The Kommos site lies unoccupied, but at the end of the period the first Greek temple (A) is founded above Minoan Building T.

1020–600 B.C. Subminoan–Greek Geometric-Orientalizing Periods. Temple B is founded above Temple A around 800 B.C. Building Q is built later. After a period of intense use, the sanctuary is largely abandoned at end of period.

600–400 B.C. Archaic/Classical Periods. Limited use. An outdoor shrine with a single built altar (H) and a building (F) of uncertain use.

400–30 B.C. Late Classical and Hellenistic Periods. Rejuvenation of the Greek Sanctuary with the founding of Temple C above Temple B, followed by the building of numerous other structures (A1, B, D, E, W), and altars (C, L, M).

30 B.C.–A.D. 150 Roman Period. Limited use followed by desertion of the site.

Chart 2. Chart Outlining the Years of Exploration of the Kommos Site

1924 Arthur Evans, excavator of Knossos, discovers the Kommos site, naming it "Komo." He does not excavate.

1965 Joseph Shaw, Ph.D. candidate at the University of Pennsylvania, first visits the Kommos site. During ensuing years he explores the area by foot and promotes an excavation project.

1976 With permit, land purchase, and funding in place, excavation by the University  of Toronto begins under the auspices of the American School of Classical Studies with the permission of the Greek authorities. During the first season three areas are sampled: the hilltop and the upper and lower hillsides. Minoan houses, part of a town, are discovered in the first two. Deep sand prevents definitive work on the lower, southern, hillside.

1977 Clearing of the overburden of wind-carried sand begins in the spring, a process that will continue at intervals for some years as additional land purchases are made south of the original land expropriation. Unexpected discoveries at the bottom of the sand accumulation in the southern area are buildings of the Greco-Roman period, including an altar, later called Altar  C. Excavation of the Minoan town to the north continues through 1983.

1978–1981 Purchase of more land to the south makes possible the discovery of a Greek temple, later called Temple C, and other buildings belonging to a Greek sanctuary, as well as three more altars in a court east of Temple C. A sounding below the  temple reveals two earlier ones (A, B), the latter with a shrine composed of three pillars, later identified as having Phoenician inspiration. Excavation into the earth level below the sand, west of and below Temple C and along the seaside scarp, exposes unexpectedly large Neopalatial Minoan architecture, a structure later dubbed "Building T."

1983–1985 After all of the Greek Sanctuary has been exposed on the upper level, excavation east of it shows that Building T extends below and to an unknown distance east of the sanctuary. Subsequent seasons explore its northern rooms, including a colonnaded stoa (later called the North Stoa) along the north side of a court (later called the Central Court).

1986–1990 Study seasons with little excavation leading up to the publication of the pottery (*Kommos* II [1990] and III [1992]) and, eventually, the Kommos area and Minoan houses (*Kommos* I, in two parts [1995, 1996]).

1991–1994 After another land purchase, excavation on the east determines the position of the eastern façade of Building T as well some of its rooms, also reveals a huge Postpalatial building (P) above it. P consists of six large parallel galleries with their open western ends facing the shoreline. Subsequent excavation clears a stoa (the South Stoa) bordering the large court along its south, revealing in the process a typical Minoan palatial court flanked by architecture along its four sides, in this case with a stoa on the north facing another on the south. Excavation of Minoan House X is completed in the meantime. Excavation at Kommos is now terminated although much still remains unexplored.

1995–present Concentration on publication of the Greek Sanctuary (*Kommos* IV, 2000), the Monumental Minoan Buildings (*Kommos* V, in press), and House X (in preparation).

PART I. THE KOMMOS SITE

Fig. 1. The shore of the Libyan Sea and the Mesara Plain from the south with the Kommos site at center right

Fig. 2. The Kommos site from the southeast

This story is wound about an ancient archaeological site, Kommos (Figs. 1–3), on the island of Crete, south of mainland Greece. Its telling is informed by the perspective of over thirty years of excavation and study. The dimensions of that experience range from the very origins of the excavation to the many problems encountered along the way, the profound excitements of discovery, the experience of the land as a residuary of the past, and always to the people of the region. They are the inheritors and guardians of the land, whether their interest is a garden plot, a grove of ancient olives that Venetians passed through, an ancient structure, or the timeless source of life in a perennial spring.

The discoveries at Kommos include a prehistoric Minoan harbor-side settlement with a series of huge successive civic buildings facing a large court. The town was established about 2000 B.C. upon earlier scattered remains, continuing until it was abandoned about eight hundred years later. Not long after, a small temple was set upon the ruins of one of the earlier structures, and thus began the history of a Greek sanctuary that was to be used for over a thousand years, until it, too, was abandoned. The area was then gradually covered by up to four meters of wind-blown sand from the neighboring beach, not to be disturbed until we began revealing some of its history. These discoveries are gradually and increasingly becoming part of the fabric of our written history of the area, bringing the past alive in numerous unusual ways.

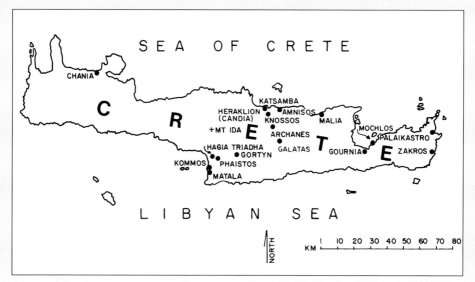

Fig. 3a

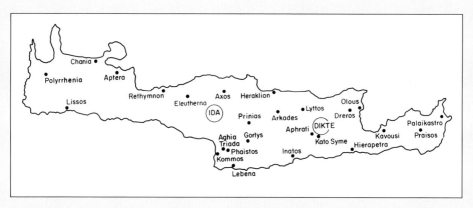

Fig. 3b

Fig. 3a. Crete, showing selected major Minoan sites

Fig. 3b. Crete, showing selected major Greek and Roman sites

THE MINOAN TOWN

At roughly the same time that the Minoan palatial culture emerged during the period known as Middle Minoan IB (MM IB; see Chart 1) extensive settlement began at Kommos. Until then the area must have been largely unsettled, with only sand accumulation and a few houses restricted to the high ridge to the south of the site (Vigles). The remains of the early Middle Minoan period (MM I/II) now lie largely obscured below later structures on the hillside. Subsequent buildings, raised during a period of prosperity (MM III) for the western Mesara, probably covered and extended beyond most of the fenced excavation area, except to the west and perhaps to the south (Fig. 4). An earthquake apparently destroyed many of these structures.

On the post-MM II hilltop (Fig. 5), one level was superimposed upon another, sometimes even mingling. In spaces 23–28, outside a later house, however, were found a series of storerooms belonging to a house. In the western one were portions of pithoi (storage jars) still in position; slabs used as bases for similar vessels lined the eastern wall. Other pots such as cups and jars, as well as common bridge-spouted vessels, were found in the eastern rooms. A part of these rooms was later covered by a Late Minoan I (LM I) court.

To the south, on the hillslope, deep layers of earth accumulation made possible excavation of a series of well-preserved, interconnecting rooms, most likely belonging to houses (Fig. 6). Many of these had two phases of floors and many contained pottery, often bridge-spouted jars placed, inexplicably, upside down. One room (48) faced south upon an open court. A Cypriot jug was found on the floor of the room next to it on the west, one of the earliest Cypriot imports to Crete and a harbinger of the period of Aegean and Near Eastern connections that was to follow. Within another room was an unusual bull's head rhyton, probably associated with ritual, done in the polychrome Kamares style (Fig. 7). Within an L-shaped storeroom (Room 25; Fig. 8) were remains crushed by the collapse of the ceiling, perhaps following a MM III earthquake. Great pithoi set on slabs lined two of the walls. Other vases had been placed near them—bridge-spouted vases and cups, and rhyta, perhaps used for ritual occasions, that included conical (Fig. 9), alabastron, ostrich egg, and piriform shapes. Around them were stone tools, most naturally rounded cobbles probably used for food preparation. These

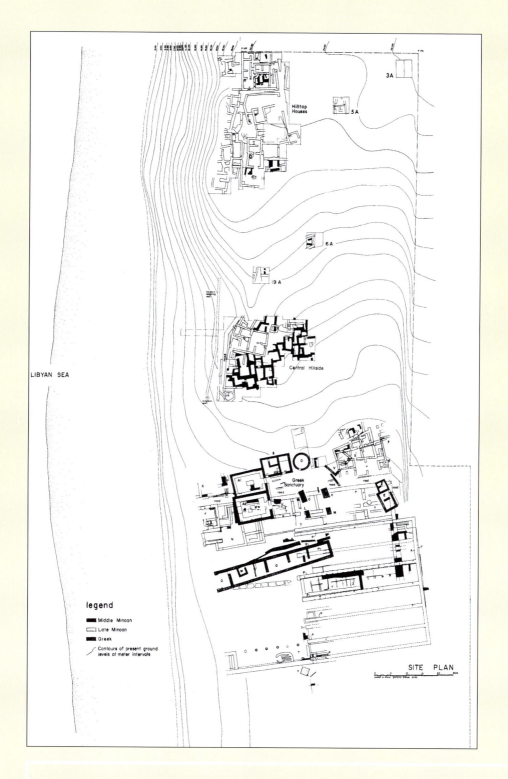

Fig. 4. Topographical plan of the Kommos site

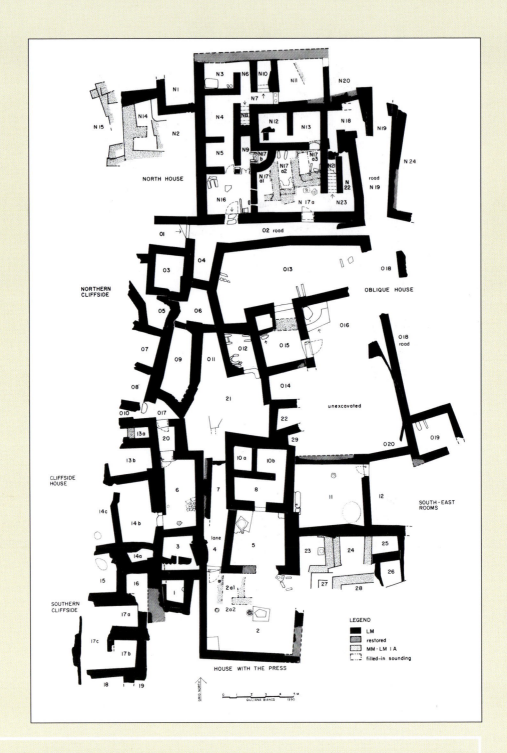

Fig. 5. Plan of hilltop houses

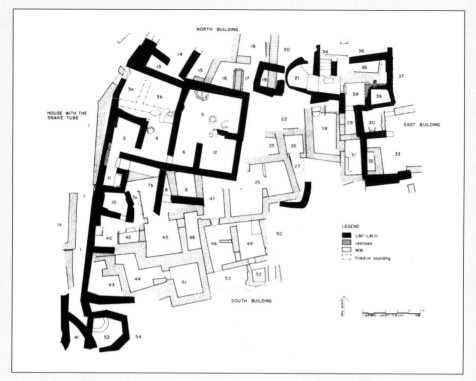

Fig. 6

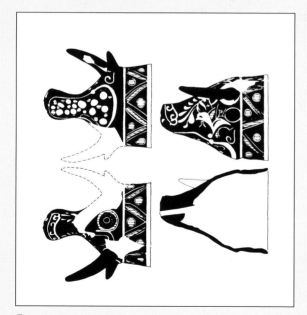

Fig. 7

Fig. 6. Plan of hillside houses

Fig. 7. A Middle Minoan bull's head rhyton from the hillside

Fig. 8

Fig. 9

Fig. 10

Fig. 8. Excavator John McEnroe in a late Middle Minoan storeroom filled with storage pithoi, other vase types, and stone tools

Fig. 9. Polychrome Middle Minoan rhyton

Fig. 10. Restored view of the North House

rooms extended eastward where reuse and erosion obscure their original appearance. While there is no clear evidence for interior stairways, numerous blocked doorways indirectly suggest access from an upper floor or even from the roof.

An earthquake seems to have brought an abrupt end to the Middle Minoan houses. Apparently the damage was so great that remodeling and reuse were not generally considered but, rather, building began from scratch after appropriate leveling. Of Late Minoan houses only a few have been cleared, although it is known that they stretch at least a hundred meters north of the fenced excavation area and some distance east, toward the modern town of Pitsidia. Within the fenced area, the use of contemporary techniques of excavation, which emphasize maximum recovery of information, has resulted in the complete clearing of a few houses. Others, partially exposed in soundings, have now been covered to protect them from the damage that follows exposure. All of the houses had a similar history, with occupation from the time of their founding in late MM III or early LM I to the abandonment of the settlement in LM IIIB, ca. 1200 B.C. The houses farthest from the shore seem to have gone out of use the earliest. What we now see are houses modified internally, with later accretions such as outbuildings. Modern walls, now covered over by a cement and earth mixture, have been built to support and protect houses and other buildings. Some scarps, especially the high ones in the southern area, have been masked with a metal mesh covered with cement and earth. Earth in many ancient walls has also been replaced by cement.

Four houses and their outbuildings have been cleared on the hilltop. These lie in a strip about fifty by twenty meters along the edge of the cliff, of which perhaps a few meters have been lost to erosion since the Minoan period. Along the east they are bordered by a north-south road (see Fig. 5, O18, N19) separating groups of houses. The northernmost house excavated, the "North House" (Fig. 10), its northern border lying just below the fence line, had over a dozen rooms. Its main entrance was from the south by means of an east-west road (O2) separating houses. The threshold, partly preserved (but with a pivot), led into a spacious room (N17) with a hearth. From here one could originally go left into rooms along the cliffside where bowls and stemmed cups (kylikes) were found, or, by turning right, one could mount the steps presumably leading to the second story (in N23). This, the largest house known on the hilltop at Kommos, was subdivided into eastern and western sections toward the end of its history, with at least three western rooms constituting a separate residence. Breaking through the southern wall provided the entrance to N16. This new entrance room had a clay hearth or small oven.

The next house to the south, dubbed "Oblique" because of its unusual orientation, once had a small open square and passageway (O4, O6, O11) leading south. Later walls, however, intended to restrict passage, blocked these. Of special interest in the Oblique House are the hearths in O12 (a kitchen?), a platform of unknown use in O15, and a large stone slab in O16, canted so as to allow drainage of liquid through a stone drain into a large, apparently private court (O13). The slab may have served as a washing or shower platform, and is one of a number in the Kommos houses.

The large block of rooms farther south is divided by a north-south lane (7, 4) that led into a court (2). An important dump of Late Minoan IIIB pottery was discovered within Room 3. Room 6, entered from the north, contained two single "pot stands" on the floor, perhaps used to support jugs (amphoras). This feature is common at Kommos where "pot stands" frequently have two or three shallow round receptacles. (For pot stands see "Domestic Economy" in Part IV.) To the west was a large room (14b), possibly a private, paved court in an early phase with a superb view of the sea, which was later subdivided. It lay south of a squarish room (13b), a workroom to judge from the bronze tools found there (chisels, an awl or needle). East of the north-south lane is a four-room group (10a–b, 8, 5) that may have been used for storage and work rather than residence. Room 5 was carefully paved and, in its northwest corner, on a platform built on the floor, is a large stone slab with a flat, basin-like depression and long, open spout (Fig. 11). This fine installation was no doubt used as a press for squeezing the juice from grapes for wine, or from olives for olive oil. The liquid would drain into a jar set under the tip of the spout, much as in present village practice. Parts of a pithos were found on the floor nearby. The room itself faced south onto the court (2). The western half of the court perhaps was covered, its flat roof supported by a single wooden column on a still preserved stone base, set next to a hearth. An adjacent room (11), not necessarily a court despite its lime and pebble floor, was supplied with a bench (a reused threshold) and a stone socket set into the floor, perhaps for a potter's wheel. An unusually fine LM rhyton (Fig. 12), probably to be connected with ritual, was found in fragments on the pavement.

Fig. 11

Fig. 12

Fig. 11. Maria Shaw and the stone press bed, used for producing wine and/or olive oil

Fig. 12. Funnel-shaped Late Minoan rhyton

Fig. 13. Ritual "snake tube" with undulating handles and conical cup set into it; upper left, detail of a bird on one of the handles

Fig. 14. Restored view of Room 4 in the House with the Snake Tube

In LM I the major hillside house, located in the central hillside, dubbed "the House with the Snake Tube," was set in above abandoned Middle Minoan rooms (see Fig. 6). The house is rectangular, except for a small extension on the south (11), a room for washing or bathing with access into neighboring rooms to the north. On the northeast there was a small outbuilding (19) facing a room with a spouted stone press similar to that on the hilltop. The house was approached from the west by a road (1) that continued both north and south (unexcavated). Two stages of its façade, as well as of the threshold leading into 3a, are visible. In Room 4, representing later use of the house, a LM III "snake tube," a religious stand with birds set on its undulating handles (Fig. 13), was found leaning against the eastern wall in a circle of other pots and a slab enclosure (Fig. 14). From there one

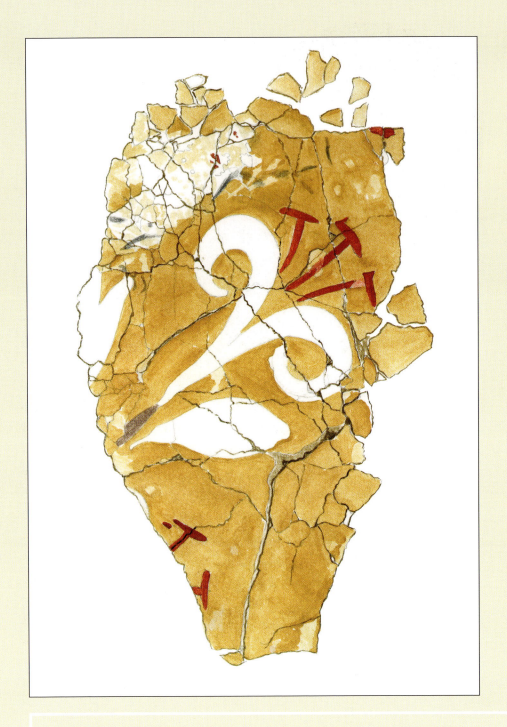

Fig. 15. Watercolor of a portion of a fresco with lilies from Minoan House X

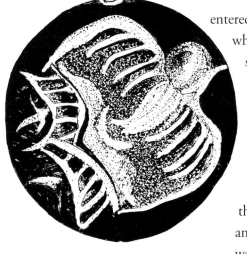

Fig. 16. Drawing of a steatite seal bead with carving of bird in flight

entered Room 6 (buried pithos below a slab), which contained an interesting series of stone tools. Room 12 was ringed by flat slabs, with a slab enclosure containing a jar, another feature common to LM III house furnishings at the site. The most interesting room is 5, perhaps partly open to the sky, with its stand that once held a cooking pot (found with the remains of insects), its two hearths, and its triple "pot stand" along the eastern wall.

Southeast of here, just north of the slab-paved Minoan road (17; see endpaper plan, upper right), is an important house dubbed "House X" with a light well (X5) open to the sky and a single column (set on a veined red limestone base), a window lighting an interior room, and a "bathing" slab within the room bordering it on the east (X6). Within and south of this room, similar to the situation elsewhere on the site, stratified sequences of pottery demonstrate the validity of proposed LM I, II, IIIA1, IIIA2, and IIIB ceramic development at Kommos. Numerous bronze tools, including knives, a sickle, and what may have been a small anvil were recovered here. So were the finest seals found during the excavation. In Room X1 we were fortunate to recover many fragments of a fresco with white lilies against a yellowish background (Fig. 15). Room X7 was a household shrine with a stone table of offerings with many jugs and shells on it; below the table were two open bowls, or kalathoi, filled with ashy material. Among the other finds were braziers and larger jugs. Of special interest was a steatite seal bead (Fig. 16). On one side is depicted with great care a bird in flight, actually perhaps a goddess in the process of becoming a bird. Surely this was an important house, perhaps linked with the functioning of the ashlar buildings to the south.

THE SOUTHERN AREA AND THE MONUMENTAL MINOAN BUILDINGS

South of the broad Minoan paved road (17, see endpaper plan), which separates houses from civic buildings, there exists above the Minoan buildings an upper, Greek layer (shown in blue on the endpaper plan). The level of its temple and altars (preserved on high podia) represents the ground level during the first millennium B.C. (in green on the endpaper plan). The pavement of the east-west Minoan road and the great Minoan court, 2.80 m below the floor of the Greek temple, orient one to the ground level during the second millennium B.C.

Some time after the founding of the Phaistos palace, during MM II, the first monumental building, called AA (in yellow on the plan), was constructed on the Kommos site. A huge level platform set on the lower slopes of the Kommos hill was built first. On the south and east, a thick wall retained it. A long covered stoa with six columns bordered the building, facing a large central court. There may have been a similar stoa along the north, but little is known about AA on either the east or west due to erosion, but also because later building razed AA to floor level. The purpose of the building is not known, but the few pottery deposits associated with it suggest a ritual use. AA might have had a predecessor to judge from a long wide walkway discovered below the court surface; the walkway (yellow in the Central Court on the plan), appears to have led from the sea on the west toward an area (building?) still unexcavated and obscured by later construction.

At about the time that the town's inhabitants were renewing their houses, they began an enormous building, "T" (Figs. 17–21), south of a broad east-west avenue that led from inland to the sea (Fig. 22), where ships would have been beached or left at anchor on calm days. T (most of the black walls south of east-west road 17 on the plan belong to it) appears to have replaced the earlier AA. T began at an eastern crossroads (now covered over). Its two high courses of cut blocks, the lower an unusually high orthostate course, rest on a projecting plinth (see Figs. 17, 18). The wall itself was probably carried up to roof level with rougher, unsquared blocks that were found fallen along the interior on the south. The façade is quite remarkable. Not only does it contain the largest blocks known to have been used in any Bronze Age building on Crete (just east of the later Greek

Fig. 17

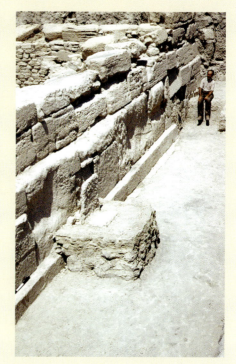

Fig. 18

Fig. 19

Fig. 17. Northwestern orthostate façade of Minoan Building T, with Maria Shaw

Fig. 18. Eastern façade of Buildings T (lower orthostates) and P (entire wall)

Fig. 19. Northeastern orthostate façade of Minoan Building T, with Alexander Shaw

Fig. 20

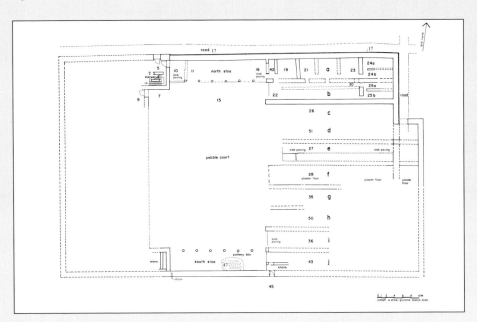

Fig. 21

Fig. 20. Restored view of North Stoa of Building T

Fig. 21. Plan of Building T

temple there is a block 0.94 m high by 3.44 m long by 0.35 m thick; see Fig. 17) but it is also the longest straight ashlar wall known from the period.

As far as one can tell this façade lacks an entrance, although farther west it joins a slightly earlier and structurally separate section of the building with a single large door leading into a slab-paved room (5) with a pier-and-door partition like those in the palaces and houses of the elite. Beyond it a stairway leads upstairs. The sea has destroyed ten meters or more of the building farther west. If it were the last building south of the road and next to the shore, as suggested in the restoration, it probably had a high north-south ashlar façade on the west.

T's Central Court is 28.64 m east-west; its north-south dimension is 39.10 m. Unlike the other great Minoan central courts which were paved with slabs (Phaistos, Knossos), packed earth or plaster (Zakros), or a combination (Malia), that at Kommos was a solid 0.20 m layering of sea pebbles brought from nearby and occasionally consolidated with lime plaster. As with palace courts, that at Kommos was intended to serve as a focus for activities carried on in the building. On its western side, already described, the entrance and a few blocks of the almost destroyed court façade continue to the south. On the north, a narrow doorway led into a broad stoa facing the court (see Fig. 20). No doubt the stoa, decorated with colorful wall painting, was meant to shelter groups of people. There were six wooden columns, each set 3.27 m from the next, on round disc-like stone bases. The stoa, called the North Stoa, was 5.20 m deep. Later building obscures much of it, but the central column base can still be seen clearly below the southeastern corner of the Greek temple. West of there, a column base foundation can

Fig. 22. Restored view of northwestern entrance to Building T and the east-west road leading to the sea

Fig. 23. Bins for grinding grain found in the North Stoa

be glimpsed through the rectangular gap left by us in the temple's modern retaining wall. To the east, below a later wall, one sees first a column base, then another foundation with a fragment of the base next to the later wall. The interior of the stoa can be inspected on the west between the temple (there is slab paving) and, on the east, where a series of bins (Fig. 23, and near no. 16 in Fig. 21), set on the original, burned paving, were probably used for grinding grain during an LM I reuse of the stoa area; later, bronze was also worked there. The pebble court is visible in front of the colonnade just described, or south of later Building Q. There the court was laid over an east-west strip of pavement of early MM date, probably a walkway leading up from the shore.

Much of the original floor plan of T just east of the court has been obscured by later construction (of "P," for which see below). East and southeast of the North Stoa, however, some of the rooms can be seen. One, a broad, long space (22) before reuse, had no obvious means of closure. It faced the pebble court and ended on the east where there were two doorways into Rooms 25a and b. Originally one would walk from the stoa into an anteroom with a double window, and then into Room 19, which was decorated with a fresco with horizontal red, black, and white stripes. Farther on were twin Rooms 24 and 25, once used for pithos storage. After a serious fire, which left a thick charcoal layer in the latter, a higher floor was set in, and at about the same time a long east-west wall was added to create "Corridor" 20, perhaps to ensure security for the room's contents. Little save cups, sherds, and a few loomweights were found on the floors. The original contents of the rooms, which appear to have been used for storage rather than residence, remain largely unknown. This eastern wing of T appears to have been of a single story. South of the area just described we have removed floors of later buildings in order to inspect floors of earlier Building T. In one place (28 on the plan) we found a long, plaster-paved floor divided by small partitions of unknown use (for drying vegetal products of some kind?). The room faced onto the court, which terminated not far to the south in the South Stoa (Fig. 24). This stoa, more visible than that to the north because later structures were not built upon it, was almost a mirror image of the North Stoa at the other end of the court. There were six columns set on bases, as in Fig. 25, and it was 5.29 m deep. On the west a flight of stairs led up to what may have been a balcony. Another stairway next to it led to the hypothetical upper floor of the wing bordering the western side of the Central Court.

Building T, of palatial proportions, comparable in size to that at Phaistos, poses questions not answered easily. If it was a palace in its own right, how could the two have been related administratively? Could a relatively small and architecturally unpretentious town such as Kommos have promoted and maintained such an enormous structure, or have we misunderstood the palaces? Perhaps they were not so rare nor served such large regions as is generally supposed. Or perhaps in T we see an adaptation of the palace form for commercial purposes rather than for religious or domestic ones. The location of T next to the shore makes this theory seem possible, all the more so since other considerations support the conclusion that Kommos served as the harbor on the Libyan Sea of Minoan Phaistos and Hagia Triada.

By the end of LM I, T was in ruins, its eastern rooms clogged with collapsed wall blocks, perhaps as the result of an earthquake. Within and near the North Stoa, however, there is evidence of reuse, probably of a domestic nature, that continued through LM II. Not long after, a new initiative of building began. Unlike the activity in LM I, during which hillside house renewal was carried out, this initiative centered on the southern area and involved the renovation of northwestern T and construction of an enormous new building.

Fig. 24

Fig. 24. View of the South Stoa area with its column bases and pottery kiln

Fig. 25. Detail of a column base from the South Stoa

Fig. 25

This LM IIIA2 renovation created Building "N" (Fig. 26, upper left), its floor a meter higher than the LM I floor. Its plan may have reflected that of T, for it had an enclosed court (6; see endpaper plan) with rooms to east and west. The court was approached up a slope from the south; a small room (4, for cooking?) was set in its northwestern corner. From the court one could enter the rooms on the east (12, 13), where bronze ingot fragments were found on the floor of the final phase. This phase was preceded by one in which a series of at least two rooms, perhaps for storage, had gone out of use. The main, western room of N (5), northwest of the court, was in what had once been part of Building T's interior. Its walls were now partly rebuilt; its floor level raised; and its northern door blocked. Like T's, N's western walls have been lost to the sea. A large, reused limestone threshold formed the building's entrance on the south.

Unlike T, which was largely empty, there was a generous distribution of intact vessels on N's floors on the northwest, presumably left when the building was abandoned, consisting of LM IIIB cups, pithoi and pithoid jars, ladles, and basins scattered inside the building and outside in the court. Both here and in the dump south of the court, wares from Sardinia testify to the internationalism of the era.

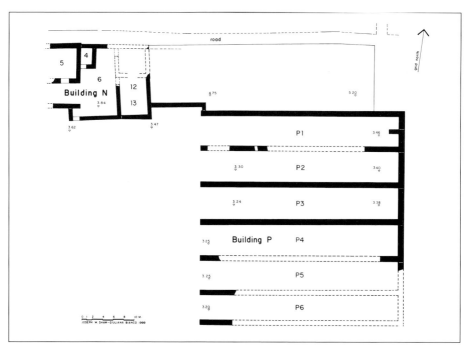

Fig. 26. Plan of Late Minoan IIIA2 Building P

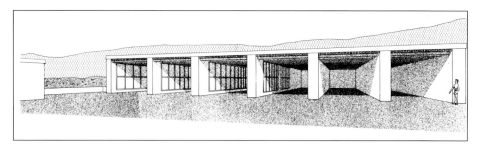

Fig. 27. Restored view of Building P

Perhaps the most curious of all buildings at Kommos is "P" (the red walls above those of T's eastern wing on the plan, also Figs. 26, 27), built over T to the southeast of N, also during LM IIIA2. Some parts of it on the southeast remain unexcavated, but enough is visible to appreciate its construction and aspects of its plan. The northern wall is particularly interesting, for thirty meters of it, up to the eastern end of T, as well as its series of east-west walls, were composed of a combination of ashlar and rubble masonry robbed from the nearby walls of Building T. At regular intervals, stout frameworks of vertical and horizontal timbers appear, a technique without close parallel elsewhere at Kommos. Perhaps the use of timber indicates an attempt to make the walls less vulnerable to earthquakes, such as the one that may have destroyed T. Beyond T on the northeast, where P was built over the north-south LM I road, the construction reverts to coursed masonry which, readily visible to passers-by, may have been intended to impress.

Parallel to and south of the northern wall of P is a series of six others at fairly equal intervals. Along their western end, next to the court, all end in coursed ashlar but, curiously, are not joined by cross walls nor are there indications that they were closed by other means. Indeed, P is composed of a series of broad, parallel galleries (as restored in Fig. 27), each about 5.50 meters or more wide and an average of 38.50 meters long. No doubt all were roofed. All share the same eastern back wall, which is actually the eastern back wall of Building T reused. During T's time, the lower part of that wall was composed of huge slabs, orthostates, set on edge and surmounted by smaller cut blocks, as along T's northern façade. These smaller blocks were probably reused in P's long sidewalls. Other large blocks from somewhere else in T were then set in above the orthostates. The huge resulting wall was thus a combination of an earlier lower course (orthostates) and at least two courses of large ashlar blocks in reuse set above them (see Fig. 18).

These galleries of P are without parallel in Minoan architecture. While their clay floors have not revealed any special features or materials, it is reasonable to expect that they were meant for storage. But storage of what in this largest Late Minoan III building known so far from Crete? Various materials known to be available, such as oil or wine (in pithoi and amphoras), grain (in sacks?), or wool have been proposed. However, the very width and open ends of the galleries must still be explained. A more convincing explanation by Maria Shaw, discussed in more detail in Part IV, is that ships of the Mesara were stored in them during the non-sailing, winter months, simply being dragged up from the neighboring shore. While analogous structures are known from Classical Greece and elsewhere, as such they would be without known parallel in the Bronze Age Aegean, but would certainly be appropriate for the size of wooden ships that the Minoans are known to have used. Eric Csapo, a former trenchmaster at Kommos, suggested that perhaps we can see this custom reflected in Homer when he refers to ships being drawn up into shipsheds some distance from the shore in the harbor of the Phaeacians (*Od.* 6.262–269). The implied distance from shore to sheds is not reflected in the known Classical Greek custom of situating the ends of the shipsheds down into the water, so may be of Bronze Age origin.

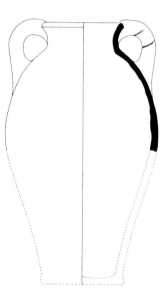

Fig. 28. A short-necked amphora from House X

Of interest in connection with the "shipsheds" is that within them were found many hundreds of fragments of two-handled storage vessels, which one of our ceramicists, L. Vance Watrous, labeled "short-necked" amphoras (Fig. 28). Few are known on Crete outside of Kommos, and they have become a vessel type localized to the Kommos site and in particular to Building P. Since such vessels could be used to export bulk products abroad, Jeremy Rutter, another of our ceramicists, is searching for them outside of Crete, so far without result.

The galleries of P, along with N and the houses, went out of use at the end of LM IIIB (ca. 1200 B.C.). Aside from occasional use during the next century, the site remained deserted until the founding of the first Greek temple, at the end of the eleventh century B.C.

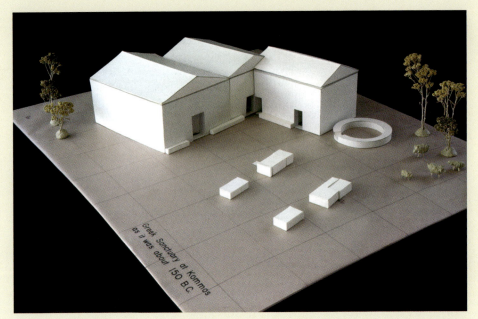

Fig. 29

Fig. 30

Fig. 29. Model of the Greek Sanctuary

Fig. 30. View of Greek Sanctuary from southeast

THE GREEK SANCTUARY (SOUTHERN AREA)

The upper, latest level of occupation in the Southern Area is that of the Greek temples and their associated buildings. The most conspicuous of the Greek buildings (Figs. 29, 30) are chronologically the latest. Of the earlier Greek buildings little is visible, chiefly because they were covered over by later structures. When excavated, naturally, the latest were uncovered first. The slab floor of the latest temple (A2 on the endpaper plan), partially removed during excavation, was replaced after the investigation of the earlier temples below.

After a period of desertion, when the earlier Minoan buildings, already covered by collapse and erosion, lay in ruins, a small simple rectangular shrine (Temple A), hardly a temple in the formal sense, was constructed around 1025 B.C. (Subminoan period). Only parts of the temple were revealed. Just as its successors would, it faced the rising sun (a normal convention of Greek temple construction). A stone sill led into it from the east; its northern wall partly reused the façade of the LM I Building T; there was probably an interior bench alongside this wall. The temple's plan does not confirm a sacral use, but the terracotta animal figurines and types of pottery found associated with it correspond to those of the later temples, built on the same spot, which were surely for ritual purposes.

After almost two centuries of intermittent use as a rural sanctuary by passersby, including occasional seamen for whom Kommos was a convenient stopping point, Temple A was succeeded by Temple B around 800 B.C. (Figs. 31, 32). This later temple was better defined and larger than its predecessor; its exterior measurements were 8.08 by 6.40 meters. Part of its western wall can still be seen running at an angle below the later Temple C. Like that of Temple A, B's roof was flat; at the center of its open eastern entranceway was a pillar. The interior featured, during its first phase, a bench 0.30 meters high (see Fig. 32) along its northern (and presumably also along its southern) wall. During its period of use it had a series of interior hearths that seem to have doubled as altars within which offerings were made, such as the terracotta figurines of horses and bulls found in the interior as well as outside in numerous dumps. Of particular interest is a shrine (Fig. 33) composed of three tapering pillars set in line next to each other and socketed into mortices cut into the top of a large triangular block (Fig. 34). It lies directly below the western column base of Temple C.

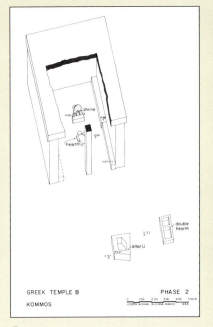

Fig. 31

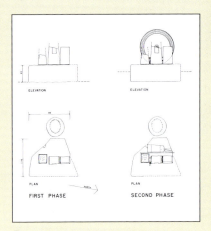

Fig. 32

Fig. 33

Fig. 34

Fig. 31. Restored Geometric Temple B

Fig. 32. Excavator John McEnroe sits on the northern bench of Greek Temple B; later hearth of Temple C is to his right

Fig. 33. Plans and elevations of two phases of the Tripillar Shrine in Temple B (the oval object behind the shrine is a wooden bowl); faience and bronze offerings, including a bronze shield, were added later

Fig. 34. Douglas Orr lifts one of the small pillars of the Tripillar Shrine; note the projecting tenon for setting it into a rectangular cutting in the stone base

Around the pillars various offerings were found: a bronze shield, seashells, a small bronze bull (Fig. 35), an unusual incised vase depicting a warrior and runners, as well as scarabs and jewelery. Other gifts were wedged between the pillars: on the south was an unusually fine bronze horse figurine (Fig. 36) upon which was set an imported Egyptian faience figurine of the goddess of war (Sekhmet, Fig. 37) and between the two northernmost pillars another faience figurine probably of her son, Nefertum. Imports from other parts of the Aegean (Attica, Corinth, and the Greek centers on what is today the shore of modern Turkey) and from the East are not unusual for this period. What is striking, however, is that beginning as early as Temple A and continuing into B's maturity, Phoenician amphora and flask fragments are found, suggesting that the Phoenicians stopped here regularly during their travels between their homeland along the Syro-Palestinian shore and their colonies far to the west. Further, although pillars are known to have been revered in Bronze Age and later Iron Age Greece, the worship of groups of tapering pillars such as those found in Temple B is known chiefly in connection with other peoples of the Mediterranean, especially the Phoenicians, leaving the impression that the Tripillar Shrine is more Phoenician than Greek in origin and, consequently, that it may be the first actual Phoenician-inspired construction identified so far in the Aegean area (see also Part IV).

External and internal changes were made to Temple B during its some two-hundred-year history. On the interior, the Tripillar Shrine was converted into the side of a hearth as the floor level rose, and at that higher level wooden benches may have replaced original stone ones. Outside, a rectangular altar, a pit or bothros in later use, came to receive the deity's portions, usually the feet or tail of the sheep and goats being consumed by the diners. Until that point the sanctuary was definitely an isolated, rural one, but at about this time, during the seventh century B.C., a small settlement appeared on a nearby hillside and at least two buildings were constructed on the east (F, V, on the plan). Low stone platforms, perhaps connected with encampment in the sanctuary courtyard, also appeared. Toward the end of this century, ca. 625 B.C., a curious, long building, Q (Fig. 38), consisting of a porch backed by a succession of rooms, was constructed south of the temple proper. Many fragments of imported transport amphoras that once probably held oil, wine, and a variety of foodstuffs were found in its rooms. Together, they suggest an unusually rich picture of trade for this period and an

Fig. 35

Fig. 36

Fig. 37a

Fig. 37b

Fig. 35. A bronze bull offering found near the Tripillar Shrine in Temple B

Fig. 36. Bronze horse, after cleaning, from Tripillar Shrine

Fig. 37. Faience figurine of Egyptian goddess Sekhmet

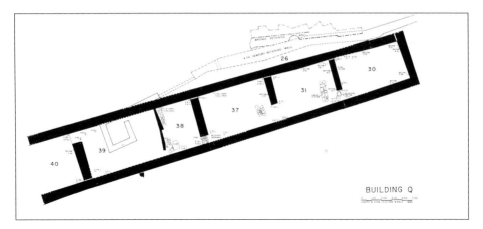

Fig. 38. Plan of Building Q, a storage depot for wines imported during the seventh century B.C.

impressive variety of commodities for use at the festivals that took place in and near the temple.

Though the sanctuary was extremely popular during the seventh century B.C., afterwards Kommos lay almost deserted for more than two hundred years. Temple B was not in use—perhaps it had collapsed—and only a small altar (part of Altar H) and occasional accumulations of pottery attest to ritual meals and sacrifice. We do not know what caused the abandonment, but a cooling of religious fervor is characteristic of many Cretan sanctuaries during the Late Archaic period. Elsewhere, as at Kommos, the Classical period heralded a revival. At Kommos, Temple C (A2 on the endpaper plan) was built, larger and better constructed than its predecessor. It had a gabled, tiled roof, with an entrance framed with Doric moldings; the temple was in the Cretan style, without either side or front columns. The side walls were almost completely removed later by stone robbers, but many of the interior features can still be seen (Fig. 39), such as the benches along the northern and southern sides (with at least three periods of enlargement). The bases of broken basins for lustration (perirrhanteria), now removed by us, supported the boards of the final benches broadened during a late phase. Roman lamps (Fig. 40) and glass containers were found on the southern stone benches. The ridge beam was supported by two stone columns set upon bases at either end of a rectangular hearth; a large, worn fragment of one of the columns lies as found in the northwestern corner of the cella, in front of the late enclosure. Along the western interior wall is a worn but once finely cut statue base, with part

Fig. 39

Fig. 39. Greek Temple C (left) and Banquet Room A1 (right) after clearing

Fig. 40. Roman lamps found in Temple C

Fig. 41. Restored plan of Temple C

Fig. 40

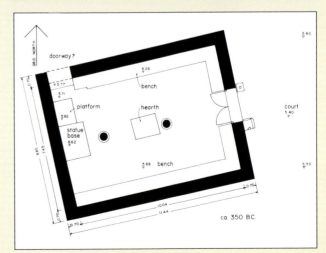

Fig. 41

of the cutting for the statue's plinth still visible in one of the blocks. A platform, perhaps for offerings, borders it on the south.

The plan of Temple C (Fig. 41) differs from that of Temple B, in that C had interior columns on axis while B was without columns although with a central axial pillar on the east. Moreover, although B had its center of worship (the Tripillar Shrine) inside, it was without C's statue(s) on an elaborate base set against the back wall. Temple C, moreover, had doors on the east, whereas both earlier temples were apparently open there. Actually, Temple C's plan derives from earlier Cretan temples of which examples have been found, as at eighth-century B.C. Dreros far to the northeast near the Gulf of Mirabello (as discussed in Part IV). The direct inspiration in the case of the Kommos temple may have been closer, perhaps at Gortyn (see Fig. 3a) where most of the early Greek levels remain undiscovered. The formal cult-statue with base (as well as base and cornice moldings), however, does not occur in earlier Cretan temples and may be at least in part a mainland custom.

When Temple C was established Altar H may have been enlarged and Altar C constructed. Burnt bones of sacrificed animals were found on both. Still standing on Altar C, facing east, was a terracotta bull figurine (Fig. 42), probably placed there by priests or pilgrims, perhaps as a substitute for an actual animal. Several additions were made gradually to the sanctuary. An intriguing round enclosure (D) was built, perhaps no higher than we see it now (see Fig. 29). Its purpose remains unknown, although we know that it had been used for cooking. Built next to it, facing onto the court, and continuing in use for a long time, was Building B (see Fig. 43), with two rooms. It was gabled and tiled, with either an attic or second story (note the well-preserved stairs in the western room). Hearths and cooking vessels in the eastern room indicate food preparation. The western room, unconnected, curiously, with that on the east, had an inner enclosure of unknown use. If there was a resident warden or "neokoros" at Kommos, Building B would probably have suited him.

Between Building B and the temple was Room A1 (see Fig. 39, right), with a central hearth and side benches that may have accommodated groups, especially diners. At first glance A1 appears to be contemporary with the temple but was actually added during the Late Hellenistic period, at about the same time that various benches were added alongside the altar court and the two southern al-

Fig. 42

Fig. 43

Fig. 42. *Greek Altar C, with the head of the bull figurine just showing (to the right and above the scale) during clearing*

Fig. 43. *Interior of Hellenistic Building B with William Cox standing on stairs leading to an upper story or attic*

tars (L, M) were built. This expansion, however, seems to have occurred not long before the site, with the exception of the temple, was deserted. The temple, probably derelict by then, was used for a while as a residence or storeroom. Not long after, a major burning of debris (ceiling beams of A2 and B?) in the court, perhaps after pillaging, turned the court floor red and singed the building façades, leaving dark soot throughout the immediate area.

This final, prosaic use of Temple C ended about A.D. 150. The sanctuary was eventually covered by sand. The cult statue or statues disappeared; only an ivory eye perhaps belonging to it was discovered. Lamps and bowls had been scattered on the interior along with a fragmentary relief of the god Pan (Fig. 44); tiles fallen from the roof and a Minoan offering bowl reused in Greek times lay abandoned, as were fragments of stone basins once used for washing and ritual cleansing. We now have only glimpses of ritual material here, similar to what was found in earlier dumps outside the temple, including bronze dress or hair pins, containers (unguentaria) for oil or perfume, wreaths composed of bronze leaves and ivory berries (Fig. 45) imitating laurel, perhaps originally set upon the cult statue. A well-preserved tripod base supported by sirens once served as a stand. Varieties of cooking, drinking, and eating wares left over from the banquets were found throughout the various stratified levels outside of the temple.

Fig. 44. Fragmentary limestone relief of Pan found in Temple C

Despite the plentiful evidence for banqueting and the large number of votives recovered from all temple periods at Kommos, the identification of the deity or deities revered there is problematic, especially for the earlier phases (as discussed in Part IV). For the later phases of Temple C we have an inscription honoring Zeus and Athena, a cylindrical altar on which Poseidon is mentioned, and the fragmentary relief of Pan (see Fig. 44) whom nymphs probably accompanied. It

Fig. 45. Watercolor of bronze laurel wreath with ivory berries recovered from outside Temple C

seems odd, however, not to find specific depictions of or dedications to these or other gods from the primary periods of Temple C or B. These gods were, therefore, possibly late additions to the principal cult. One must note in this regard that unlike many other Cretan sanctuaries, both Temples A and B lack a clear tradition of anthropomorphic iconography. A partial explanation for this absence may lie in the mute character of the "Phoenician" Tripillar Shrine (see Fig. 33) set in when B was founded, for the three pillars could represent "aniconic" deities. It might appear inconsonant to find foreign elements playing such a major role in a sanctuary with so much obvious local participation, but perhaps the Cretans displayed the same flexibility in adopting foreign practices as they did in borrowing the motifs of Eastern art. Moreover, a foreign trinity could have been accepted in a culture with similar triads, such as that of Apollo, Leto, and Artemis, recognized in Crete at Gortyn and elsewhere. There, however, the individual deities were actually depicted.

KOMMOS AND THE SEA

Unlike the remainder of Crete's south coast, the shoreline of the western Mesara, from its southern projection at Cape Lithinos some 15 kilometers north to the modern town of Hagia Galene, is roughly north-south (see Figs. 1, 46). Aside from a stretch with precipitous cliffs on the south, the remainder is open beach washed over diagonally by constant waves when the northwestern trade wind is blowing during the summer. The largest waves are those built up by an onshore west wind, usually during the winter months. Unless protected by modern encircling breakwaters (as at Kokkinos Pyrgos and Hagia Galene in the north) there is little shelter for ships. Nor was there in antiquity. For Roman Gortyn and nearby

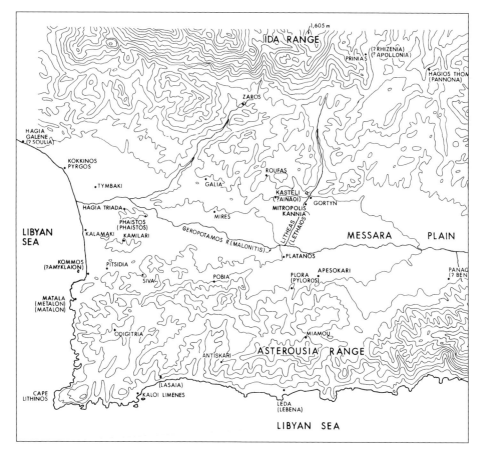

Fig. 46. Map of the western Mesara Plain

Fig. 47. Greco-Roman harbor of Matala in 1972, before its tourism acme

Classical Phaistos, the chosen harbor site was Matala (Fig. 47), south of Kommos, a fact confirmed both by historical texts and archaeological discovery. Little of the harborfront at Matala has been revealed, only a large, partly submerged platform in the center of the harbor near the shore (interpreted by some as a Roman quay of concrete) and, along the southern side of the harbor, behind a line of restaurants, an enormous vertical cutting in the seaside cliff, some 20 m long and about 5 m wide—this must be a "shipshed," probably of the Late Hellenistic or Early Roman period, into which a single warship could be pulled up a ramp, where it would be tied, ready to be launched out against any attack by armed ships approaching the harbor from the open sea.

But Matala could never have been a secure harbor for anchoring ships—even now the few fishing boats frequenting the harbor are pulled up on shore during the winter. In the other seasons, their skippers must be constantly aware of high seas that may build up during a west wind. So during the Classical Greek and Roman periods, although Matala was closer to Gortyn or Phaistos, harbors further south along the east-west shoreline (such as Kaloi Limenes and Lebena [modern Lendas]) must have been preferred for long-term shelter. As far as the prehistoric period is concerned, despite extensive surface survey and recent excavations by the Greek authorities, no Minoan remains have been reported at Matala.

This might appear odd to some, for a general (and apparently erroneous) assumption is that the Greeks always preferred U-shaped harbors. The harbors of ancient Athens (Zea, Katharos, Munychia) were of this type. To make them safe from intruders from the sea, piers were built out into the water on each side of the harbor entrance, and chains were stretched between them so as to impede entrance. This so-called closed harbor type was definitely employed during periods of strife, and was emulated later by the Romans. There were also "inner harbors" that could be created by opening up and dredging out areas along the shore so that, as for example at Carthage in Tunisia or Lechaion near Corinth, entrances could be created leading into protected harbor basins. To date, however, no convincing prehistoric examples, Minoan or Mycenaean, have been reported from the Aegean area.

At this stage in harbor research, it appears that two types were preferred during the Bronze Age. One, like Hagia Irini on the island of Kea, was on either side of a peninsula that projected out into the sea. In that case much of the town was

Fig. 48

Fig. 49

Fig. 48. Mochlos islet, once linked to the shore by a spit of land

Fig. 49. Amnisos harbor with the remains of Minoan houses awash

Fig. 50. The "Papadoplaka" reef in the distance off the Kommos shoreline; during Minoan times it projected out of the water significantly more

erected on the peninsula, and the shoreline on either side was used for pulling up the ships. In calm weather vessels could also be anchored offshore. Depending on the direction of the wind, ships could be brought in on one side or another of the peninsula. A similar situation may have existed at Mochlos in northeastern Crete (Fig. 48), where a spit of land, once linking the present island to the shore, is now under water. Another type of harbor seems to have been one with a fairly open, broad beach with a small offshore islet. This was the case with Amnisos (Fig. 49), one of the two harbors of Knossos (Fig. 3a), north of Kommos.

It was also true of Kommos, for some distance offshore a reef projects above the waterline and breaks the force of the waves (Fig. 50). The reef is called locally the "Papadoplaka," "the priest's slab," for no known reason. During antiquity the reef would have appeared considerably larger, for not only was the relative water level lower and the coastline farther out during the Minoan period, but the islet itself has been reduced in size by Nazi planes making practice bombing runs during World War II. Geologist John Gifford believes that there was probably a sandy spit or tombolo linking shore with islet, giving ships shelter for anchorage and dissipating the strength of the waves. Usually, however, ships could simply be drawn up alongside each other on the shore.

The geological morphology of the Kommos shoreline has played an equal role in the appearance of the site today. When Neopalatial Building T was constructed, we believe it featured, like many other palatial Minoan structures, a large west wing. That wing is now gone, erased by the force of the waves that undermined the walls and pulled them down into the sea. Only a small stretch of façade along the Central Court remains of what must once have been a significant complex of rooms, perhaps as much as 40 meters wide east to west. This change in relative water level, we think, took place at the transition from the LM IIIA1 to LM IIIA2 ceramic periods when the great buildings N and, especially, P (see Figs. 26, 27) were constructed. Part of T on the northwest, next to the shoreline, was still standing and its walls were reused in Building N. Particularly evident regarding the relative water level at the time is the fact that T's rooms were filled in, their earlier floor level being raised at least a meter, an unnecessary exercise if the water level had remained unchanged. Of course, we are referring to the maximum height and horizontal "reach" of the waves as they approached the shore. The actual height of sea level at the time was considerably below the bottom of the walls.

Direct evidence for interaction with the sea at the site varies. The simplest are the many bronze fishhooks, barbed and unbarbed, from both Bronze Age and Iron Age contexts. To judge from the number of hooks found in Minoan House X, surely inhabitants ventured out in their boats from the shore. We also recovered a bronze object thought to be a net mender from a dump south of Greek Temple C. Then there are masses of fish bones, especially from the Greek temple deposits and hearths that were recovered using wet and dry sieving techniques. Although most of the identified fish are smaller ones from relatively shallow waters (e.g., sea bream, wrasses, parrot fish, mullet), angel sharks, sea bass, and tuna from deeper waters were recovered as well. Of man-made artifacts, numerous "loomweights" (Fig. 51), usually associated with weaving but also used as weights for fishing nets, were found. About a dozen stone weights that could have been used as anchors were also discovered. Mostly, these examples can be dated to the Bronze

Fig. 51. Terracotta loomweights from House X, used for fishing as well as weaving

Age, including the two Syrian anchors, each weighing over a hundred pounds, that were found in reuse within one of the long galleries of Building P (see Part III). The fanciest anchor, however, was a partially preserved marble anchor stock, 60 centimeters long, found in fragments within and outside of Temple C. Very few pieces of marble were found, so that special note was taken when these were recovered. At first, when two fragments appeared, their identification as the stock (an upper part) of a Classical anchor was unsure; but then, years later, another joining piece was recovered, reused in a Hellenistic Greek wall. The identification could then be confirmed. Since marble is easily dissolved by constant exposure to seawater, this anchor may have been votive in nature, perhaps dedicated by a thankful fisherman after a narrow escape or a successful catch at sea.

The most common foreign artifacts, of course, are fragments of pottery. Representing the Bronze Age are some from Cyprus, Egypt, Syria-Palestine, and Sardinia (e.g., those in Figs. 52, 53). For the Greek period there are numerous fine wares from exporting cities such as Athens and Corinth. Also there are transport amphoras used for wine, and other wares from the Greek city-states along the present shores of modern Turkey. Many were found in connection with Archaic Building Q, which seems to have functioned as a storehouse for the wine consumed by the participants in ritual dining and sacrifice carried out inside Greek Temple B. Some of them, as well as the rare Phoenician wares, are discussed in more detail in Part IV.

Of course mysteries remain, which is appropriate when dealing with the sea. The waters off Kommos remain shallow until one is some distance from the shore. At a point a few hundred meters from the shore, it is said by local fishermen that there is a long built wall connecting the projecting reef, the "Papadoplaka" (see Fig. 50), with a monstrous boulder to the south (called "Volakas"). The boulder is so large that, according to the fishermen, it could only have been thrown to where one sees it now, in fairly deep water, by the great one-eyed Cyclops who, some say, lived in a nearby cave on shore. Of the wall, said to be standing in about eight meters of water, however, we have seen nothing even after snorkeling alongside a fisherman in his boat, who was pointing out where he had seen the "wall." If such a wall is ever found, our geomorphologists will have a real challenge to explain it.

Fig. 52

Fig. 53

Fig. 52. Conservator Kathy Hall completes restoration of a large Late Minoan III Cypriot pithos found in Minoan House X

Fig. 53. Sardinian collar-necked jar from Late Minoan IIIB context on the hilltop

Another mystery to be untangled is that concerning Menelaos's wreck, for Homer tells how part of Menelaos's fleet, on its return from Troy, was blown off course to the southern coast of Crete

> . . . where the Kydonians lived around the streams of Iardanos. There is the sheer of a cliff, a steep rock out in the water at the other end of Gortys on the misty face of the main, where the south wind piles up a huge surf on the left of the rock horn toward Phaistos, and a little stone holds out the big water. It was there they came, and by lively work the men avoided destruction, but the waves smashed their ships on the splinters of rock, but the wind and the water catching up the other five dark-prowed ships bore them along and drove them on Egypt.
>
> (*Od.* 3.292–300)

Years ago a wreck was spotted along the cliffs to the south in three or four meters of water. It is still visible from the cliffs above, but less easy to discern when one is actually snorkeling below. The pottery, however, even though partly covered by sea growth, looks more recent. So Menelaos's wreck(s) still remains to be found. This raises the possibility of finding an ancient wreck in the deeper water along the Nisos Peninsula and south to the tip of Cape Lithinos where the Cretan coast resumes its east-west direction. Surely there are deepwater wrecks there that would more than repay investigation, of ships that were beating up against the wind, attempting to reach the Matala or Kommos harbors, but were crushed against projecting cliffs. These Greek or Minoan wrecks with, hopefully, intact cargos, such as those found recently off the coast of Turkey at Cape Gelidonya and Uluburun, could be a major event in Cretan nautical archaeology, a discipline still in its infancy.

PART II. PITSIDIA AND THE WESTERN MESARA

Fig. 54. The town of Pitsidia in 1978, before its expansion

The landscape of excavations varies considerably. If in a built-up urban area, such as the city of Chania in western Crete, archaeological investigation is likely to be conducted within the rectangular confines of a house plot, excavated because, by law, building cannot take place unless any antiquities in the plot are investigated. Ancient houses found there, Minoan, Greek, Roman, and later, have differing orientations and sizes, but the same general arrangement: an ancient pattern seen within a contemporary frame.

In the countryside the circumstances are different. In non-developed areas with few paved roads, but with tracks, walking is the best approach. Archaeologists "read" such landscapes by foot, by searching the land for evidence of past use. Broken pottery, from a time before the use of glass or tin, provides the only residue of what has passed over it. One can savor the land in this way. Occasionally one is lucky enough to find architecture—the line of a wall, a cut block or slab, a threshold block. But most often it is the pottery, broken and discarded, that provides the key to habitation. Pottery is able to provide such useful clues because during various prehistoric and historic periods pots had different shapes and designs, as well as surface treatments, that can be identified by those who have spent time familiarizing themselves with that history. Experts claim that the styles of some Minoan pottery can be differentiated in terms of the decades during which they were made—Late Minoan II, for instance. The history of the Mesara Plain, with Kommos located in one corner, is still being written by the study of these remains, sometimes exposed, sometimes masked by earth, bushes, or sand near the broad western shoreline.

The "archaeological landscape" of urban centers within the Mesara Plain, such as Phaistos or Gortyn, consisted at the time we began our exploration of clusters of houses connected by tracks and paths, occasionally by paved roads, all surrounded by the fields that had always provided sustenance. Roads, now paved with asphalt, had long led from Venetian Mires to Petrokephali to Pitsidia, and on to Matala. It would be Pitsidia on this track that became our summer home for thirty years.

THE PITSIDIA/MATALA COMMUNITY

Pitsidia (Figs. 46, 54–60) is a small town on the main route to Matala, the end of the bus line. Historically the two towns, close to one another, have been a single administrative unit, with an elected mayor and a council to advise him, until being forced recently, under the rules of the European Union, to be absorbed into a much larger unit. Some have posited, due to the town's name, that refugees from Pisidia in Turkey may have founded Pitsidia, but that is purely speculative. The old main road through the town now skirts the small town square, once replete with cars and buses parked at every imaginable angle and the site of social gatherings (Fig. 57) but now filled with restaurant tables. Facing the square are three restaurants, three "rooms-for-rent" buildings, a kafeneion and a kafeteria (a somewhat upgraded kafeneion). About seven hundred people live in the town, which has been growing in size as it spreads out—to the east around the hillside on which it is nestled and toward the neighboring town of Siva from where on a Sunday one can hear the church bells ringing across the hills.

On the west is the main road, put in about thirty years ago, along which a small hotel and half a dozen restaurants have sprung up, often with rooms for rent on the upper floors and usually housing the establishment's owners, as well as a state-of-the art bakery with rows of delicacies and great stainless steel ovens and machinery. West of the road is Melanouri, a hillside with a view of the distant sea, where retirees and successful merchants have recently been building comfortable houses. Despite Pitsidia's new lateral expansion, however, its population has remained relatively stable over the years. As some of the young people have moved to Herakleion and elsewhere, retirees have filled the gaps left. Still, even in the center of the town there are abandoned buildings with collapsed roofs held up partly by broken, rotting timbers. There are two small churches along the town's southern border, near the small town hall, next to which is the town spring that has been polluted, I was told, by septic tanks leaking into the water source. Now water is pumped into the village from below the local water table; it is too laden with dissolved lime to be drinkable, and, like so many other areas in the Mesara Plain and elsewhere in Crete, bottled water is brought in from unpolluted sources high on the hillsides of the Idaian Mountains that border the Mesara along the north.

Fig. 55. The court of the excavation storage area in Pitsidia where study of stone tools and pottery took place, with Harriet Blitzer

Fig. 56. Pitsidia storeroom with Maria Shaw and Niki Kantzios

Fig. 55

Fig. 56

I first saw Pitsidia close-up from the back of a motorcycle when, in 1970 or so, Phaistos guard Zacharias Spyridakis, who first directed me to the then isolated Kommos site, stopped at a kafeneion along the road. This was during the period of the Papadopoulos dictatorship, which lasted from 1967 to 1974. The mayor then was Manolis Kyprakis, a gracious and enthusiastic man who welcomed (I thought at the time) Zacharias's impolitic comment about future excavation along the shore. The second time I visited Pitsidia was in 1975 when it became clear that the excavation storage and accommodation was to be centered in the town. At one point two other possibilities had been entertained, both of which would have been disastrous if they had been attempted. One was Matala (see Fig. 47), where in the late 60s the town was still almost deserted before a hippie invasion was followed by hotels, restaurants, souvenir shops, and "rent-rooms" that catered to those coming to see the hippies, many of whom lived along the shore, others under the trees or in caves in the great striated limestone cliffside. The caves actually were once Roman tombs, quite filled with body-sized carved sarcophagi, and with burial gifts such as pottery and terracotta lamps. Another possibility for excavation headquarters was at Kommos itself, in the southern part of the property being acquired. We even made a fine plan of a building with rooms opening onto a central courtyard. During the winter months, however, when the shore is typically deserted, any structure there would have been broken into and ransacked, so that plan was also abandoned. The Pitsidia building chosen for a base (see Figs. 55, 56) originally had three rooms (later expanded to four), one to be used for drafting, study, and (eventually) for a small usable library, with the other two being filled with metal shelves chiefly for the storage of pottery (our main small find), stone tools, artifacts, shells, and the like, all labeled according to their exact provenance on the site. The large court, filled with movable tables used during the day for pottery sorting (see Fig. 55), would be shaded in the future by vine-covered shelters and a great pine tree. The owner of the house had died in the process of its being built and we completed it, along with the once temporarily roofed septic tank into which one of our team fell but was rescued after his pitiful shouts for help brought aid. Thus we were living in that town, "commuting" to the archaeological site, and working with the very heirs of the ancient land that we had come to explore. Instead of living in splendid isolation in an English-speaking compound of some type, we joined the present community which still belongs to the land, a continuation of the past whether it be Minoan, Greek, Byzantine, or Venetian.

Beginning in 1976, our international staff began arriving, men and women, advanced academics, geologists, botanists, faunal experts, linguists, technicians, students of ancient culture, all usually chosen on a competitive basis, all usually with transportation, room and board paid, the technicians with salaries. Those who would go into the field as trenchmasters were chosen for their ability to maintain impeccable trench notebooks and, at the end of the season, to complete full, illustrated reports. Those mostly working in Pitsidia—cataloguers, a photographer, an excavation architect, pottery profilers—were chosen for their capabilities and their compatibility. Some were with us for many seasons. The "Pitsidia" staff would walk the few kilometers to the site shortly before we quit in the afternoon, inspect our progress in the trenches, and then go for a swim at what some called, with pride, "the best beach in the Aegean," some venturing out as far as the Papadoplaka (see Fig. 50). Later, dinner was prepared and served in Pitsidia by local cooks who became members of our family. All of us sat at a single long table that expanded or shrank depending on staff size.

Fig. 57. The town square of Pitsidia after a celebration

And there were celebrations (as in Fig. 58). In the middle of the season, coinciding with the Director's birthday, a secretly prepared issue of the excavation newspaper, *The Mesara Message*, was produced. Everyone contributed an article, a cartoon, a spoof. It was, and still is, the only English newspaper (circulation 35) published in the Mesara. In one issue, as a response to the volume of legs of votive bulls found in the Greek levels, without their (more friable) upper bodies, our excavation architect, Giuliana Bianco, suggested in a cartoon that all the legs actually belonged to an ancient Greek statue of a millipede. A yearly series depicted the exploits of our hero figure, "LM Man," brilliantly drawn by our chief cataloguer at the time, Niki Holmes Kantzios (Fig. 56): LM Man protected the poor against the overweening rich and audacious.

Fig. 58. Musicians at a party in Pitsidia

Wives and children participated as well, although usually their accommodations were separate. John, Michael, and Mary Betancourt did much of our shopping in crowded Mires; Alexander and Robin Shaw (Figs. 19, 24, on the furthest column base), who came as children, graduated to workman status; Nick Rutter's drawings and cartoons also enlivened *The Mesara Message*. And there were marriages galore among the staff! At least six that I can recall, all during the first decade of work when the cycles of discovery on the site created fast friendships, and since then not a single divorce among those.

Over the thirty years of excavation we must have employed at least three hundred villagers, from the time of the Greek drachma to that of the present Euro. Many of our earliest, best workmen have passed on. Their children, and then their grandchildren, often replaced them. We know many of the Pitsidia families as a result, generation after generation, and have been grateful for their friendship and hospitality.

A major effect of the excavation has been on the landscape. As soon as it was clear that there was an ancient town at the Kommos area along the shore, almost the entire area from the new modern road west to the shoreline, a distance of at least a kilometer, was declared by the Archaeological Service to be in the "A" category, namely that new building was not to be allowed. Thus the Archaeological Service has played a role in controlling development. There has essentially been no building since that time. In the only case when it was attempted (by a speculator from nearby Mires), the equipment (e.g., timber and steel reinforcing) was confiscated twice by the Archaeological Service, and the area that he cleared along the cliffside with a bulldozer may possibly become a public parking lot when the site is opened to the paying public in the future.

While the larger area affected by the edict remained open and pristine (see Fig. 1), with sandy hillsides, fig trees, irregular patches of vineyards, those who owned property within it complained mightily. Part of their inheritance had, in effect, been declared invalid. There is still understandable bitterness among many.

Events accompanying a property transfer in 1990 brought things to a head. What occurred was the result of our speculation that the enormous structure (Building T; see Part I) that we had been unveiling parts of over the past years actually had the form of a Minoan palace, with a huge central court with "wings" on all four sides. At the time we had found the northern part of the large court and a colonnaded stoa facing south onto it (see Fig. 20), along with what could possibly be interpreted then as the northwestern corner of the court. All of this was bordered along the north by a massive ashlar façade, one of the longest such monumental façades in Crete, next to a paved east-west road that we think also connected with the chief road from inland Phaistos to the sea (see Fig. 22). The façade then continued eastward an unknown distance beyond our property line. We thus planned to acquire a fairly large portion of land extending south and east. The problem in laying out the border of that area was that, since this was to be our third and final land purchase, we had to be relatively sure that the eastward bound façade wall "cornered" within the new property, and would still leave room on the east for the enormous scarp that would result, almost ten meters high, when we had excavated the sloping ground down through the meters of sand to the ancient level. The extension to the south, on the other hand, had to be sufficient to allow us to "capture" the still hypothetical extension of the Central Court as well as an unseen south wing. A calculation was made, therefore, based on the relative size of the central courts and south wings of the four known Minoan palaces, a bit of leeway was added, and the new property markers went in. The purchase was made in cash in Athens in the spring.

Returning to Pitsidia, not long afterward, with the aim of enclosing the new land with a fence, I found other forces in motion. One was a group of topographers representing

Fig. 59. Village characters of Pitsidia

the former owner who wanted to be sure that we didn't enclose any land that belonged to their client. Another was a group that claimed that the land we had purchased actually belonged to them and not to the person to whom we had made payment. Still another group represented a man claiming to own a good portion of the hillside bordering the site on its south (and then some). So there were at least four groups involved, some with surveying instruments, others with pipes and posts being used as property markers, with strings stretching in all directions.

To make matters worse, the then mayor of Pitsidia set a front loader to work extending a new road along a sand track from the village to near the shoreline, making a great diagonal path across the property we had just bought. Gravel was brought in as well. He called it a "public road," claiming its inviolability and suggesting that we might want to excavate on either side (which would have been impossible). There were strong feelings on all sides, and my foreman George Beladakis suggested that I keep my head low. But what to do? The "public road" presented a real problem. I called our lawyer Harry Bikakis in Athens. "Put in the fence," he advised, "put in the fence." This I did, for the fence contractor had come and was awaiting instructions. In the meantime I had the mayor's approval to move the access road outside the property/fence line; the topographers representing the owners also gave their approval for a narrow road on "their" property. Then, in half a day, the fence and gate went in, and the diagonal "public road" along with its gravel was removed, to be repositioned outside the fence line. Thus public access to the shore was maintained and we were free to begin excavation,

Fig. 60. A Pitsidian house

which lasted on a large scale until 1995. I am relieved that that was our last land purchase.

As excavation progressed, the southern border of the Central Court, with a fine colonnaded stoa, was found (see Fig. 24; Parts I and IV). At the same time that the site was becoming more impressive, each day, but especially on the weekends, dozens and dozens of cars bound for the beach came, usually filled with shore-bound local inhabitants. At about the same time one of the most innovative Pitsidia mayors, a former teacher, Michalis Kotsifakis, took charge. Kotsifakis had a vision of Matala as a carefully developed tourist/commercial center and the Kommos area as an "archaeological park." It was during Mayor Kotsifakis's tenure that my wife Maria and I had our greatest accolade when we were made honorary citizens of the town of Pitsidia. He had prepared a specially decorated diploma using Minoan pottery designs and emblems of the sea. The Ephor (or Director) of Antiquities of the Herakleion province, Alexandra Karetsou, made a moving address about Kommos being the ancient gateway to southern Crete, and there was a high banquet put on for the occasion. Our duties: none. "Our" village in Crete.

Kotsifakis's idea conformed well to our own view. A visiting conservation planner from Colorado, James Stratis, began a study detailing areas on the site where lookouts over the excavated area and/or the sea might be established, finding paths that visitors could take, where dangerous areas could be fenced off, and areas where future excavation could take place. Drainage along the east, next to the access road, was of particular concern, for torrential winter rains could collapse the ten-meter-high eastern scarp. A special visitor's center and guardhouse was planned for the main entrance, on the southeast; it would be in the shape of a ship, representing the role of the site in Bronze Age commerce. Parking areas were also suggested. This was submitted to the Greek authorities in 1998. It was resubmitted, along with a program of consolidation walls and scarps, in 2001. We were given permission to do the latter, an expensive job, now well underway. The original request we still await word on. That role, naturally, will be the Greek Government's, which will take over the site on a permanent basis as soon as conservation is complete. This would be most welcomed by the Pitsidians who would benefit especially from the tourism that it would attract. The Kommos site is a large one with much to see and consider; at the same time the neighboring beach, wide and beautiful, extends south to the high cliffs where there are restaurants and continues north (see Figs. 1, 46) a kilometer to Kalamaki, with its recently developed line of attractive shore-side restaurants.

THE WESTERN MESARA

The fertile Mesara Plain (see Fig. 46), the largest in Crete, extends some thirty-five kilometers east-west, from the foothills leading east to the Viannos area to the Libyan Sea on the west. There a wide sandy shoreline borders the plain, stretching from sandy Kommos on the south to rocky Kokkinos Pyrgos on the north. Some ten kilometers wide at its center, the Mesara is enclosed on the south by the high, now dry hills of the Asterousia range, with occasional precipitous access to anchorages at Tsoutsouros, Lendas, and Kaloi Limenes. Matala (see Fig. 47) on the southwest (due south of Kommos) is also a fair harbor, opening on the west. Along the plain's northwestern edge towers the high range of Ida, the mythical birthplace of Zeus, which as it goes east becomes hills gradually merging with a plateau bordering the plain. The chief access to the north nowadays falls west of the Platiperama Valley, itself northeast of Gortyn. In antiquity several more easterly routes gave access to the north.

The eastern part of the plain, drained by the eastward flowing Anapodaria (ancient Potherious) River, often dry, reflects the general settlement pattern; towns are established at intervals along the edges of the plain where sources of water, pasture, and arable land are accessible. The western part of the plain, nourished by waters flowing south from the Idaian range, is drained by the Geropotamos River (ancient Malonitis), a perennial stream that disappears into a swampish, alluvial area at the shore of the Libyan Sea. Lately the Geropotamos has often been dry, as pumps throughout the plain draw water for agriculture and for towns scattered along its edges and two large central towns, Mires (pop. over 2,200) and Tymbaki (pop. over 2,800), where people have concentrated. Opinions differ as to whether the Malonitis was ever navigable; the presence of harbor towns representing both major ancient periods (Minoan and Greco-Roman) along the present shoreline, however, suggests that it was not. Throughout its post-Roman history Crete had few political or commercial relations with North Africa. As a partial result, access to the island since the Roman period has not been via the Libyan Sea, but, rather, by means of the gentler, more accessible northern coast. Even now vegetables, fruit, and grain grown in the Mesara are exported principally to northern markets, usually via Herakleion, and in turn manufactured goods are sent south from Herakleion to the Mesara.

Although no intensive archaeological survey has yet been carried out in the eastern Mesara, it is nevertheless clear that settlement in the plain was concentrated in the west. Before the beginning of the Minoan palatial period, ca. 2000 B.C., there was scattered Final Neolithic and Early Minoan occupation at Kommos, and Late Neolithic settlements somewhat inland at Phaistos and also just east and south of it. In the subsequent Early Minoan period (ca. 3000–2000 B.C.) numerous circular tombs indicate the existence of several small towns in the foothills south of the Geropotamos and, especially, in the higher southern hills (the first and last time that the latter were thickly settled). The Palatial Age then brought about a number of changes, largely, it seems, as a result of a little understood development in social organization throughout Crete, which led to the founding of large local civic centers, usually called "palaces." The Phaistos palace (Fig. 61), which was to endure in its basic plan with rebuilding until ca. 1450 B.C., was located directly upon earlier houses set on that high limestone hill rising from the plain. The ensuing period of peaceful development brought with it the establishment of numerous smaller settlements west of Phaistos, including some either on the shore (as at Kommos), or not far from the shore (as at Hagia Triada; Figs. 3a, 46, 62), also in MM I. At Kommos there were houses on the hilltop and

Fig. 61. The Minoan palace of Phaistos

the hillside (described in Part I). Scrappy remains of contemporary buildings, also presumably houses, lie below the later civic buildings to the south.

Most scholars believe that the palaces were centers for administration and collection of local produce, and served as residences for those responsible for the administration of the economy. While little is known of the structure of government then, it may not have led to any seasonal armed combat between centers. Phaistos and Knossos, for instance, lack clear evidence of major defensive walls. Conditions favored agriculture, an increase in population, and, probably, the development of trade. Following a major destruction, the Phaistos palace was partially rebuilt ca. 1700 B.C. with great skill on a revised but similar plan around a large central court. At about the same time two or more luxurious dwellings were built at Hagia Triada (Fig. 62), their residential areas with appointments as sophisticated as any elsewhere in Crete. Parts of them have been discovered almost intact as they were abandoned in a conflagration ca. 1450 B.C., a period when Phaistos and many other Minoan sites, but apparently not Kommos, suffered similar destruction.

Not long after the Phaistos palace was partially rebuilt, there was renewed activity at Kommos. Houses were set over the remains of the earlier ones on the hilltop and part of the hillside. These were relatively small, as their predecessors had been, without the alabaster revetment or ample storerooms and work areas of the elite seen at neighboring Hagia Triada. Rather, they were comfortable without being luxurious, more like the humble houses of farmers and fishermen. One of these, however, House X to the south, seems to have been special, with a light well and at least one room decorated with a colorful fresco with lilies (see Fig. 15). Also, a major building operation was begun south of an east-west road (17 on the endpaper plan), on the more level area behind the shoreline, south of the hillside, above Building AA discussed briefly in Part I. Building T was a civic building, perhaps one constructed as a result of an initiative begun at Phaistos and Hagia Triada, the presumed ruling centers in the area at the time.

The mid-fifteenth century B.C. was one of transition in Crete. A major change in rule seems to have taken place; Phaistos was burned and largely abandoned, as were Hagia Triada and most other palace sites, with the possible exception of Knossos, which some scholars believe to have brought about the upheavals in a successful bid to extend or consolidate its rule. In the Mesara, the Kommos

Fig. 62. The settlement and villa at Hagia Triada before being covered by a protective roof

houses, however, continued to be inhabited, as did the stoa area of Building T which itself had suffered partial burning and collapse some time before. The pottery style in use then, LM II or "Palace Style," has been found throughout the site, for which see Part IV.

On many Minoan sites the period after LM I was one of total or partial disuse. In the Mesara, Phaistos was nearly abandoned but partially regained its importance ca. 1150 B.C. At Kommos and Hagia Triada, however, the pattern was different. At the former, a new major building, "P" (see Figs. 26, 27), was built in LM IIIA2, perhaps the largest construction of its time in Crete. With its enormous galleries which appear to be designed for the storage of goods or ships, P represents a major renewal of harbor facilities in a town that can be shown, by the pottery found, to have had trade connections with Syria and Cyprus to the east and, later, with Sardinia to the west. At the same time that P was built, part of T, the building known as N, was reused at a higher level. N consisted of a series of rooms set about a small court, an arrangement reminiscent of the earlier palaces. Although during its final use in LM IIIB it was probably a residence, its plan suggests that it may have been an administration building connected with activities in nearby Building P.

Despite the renewals and changes, the general nature of the activity at Kommos seems to have remained consistent, with residence in the relatively small houses to the north and commerce in the huge earlier buildings to the south. At Hagia Triada, however, there had also been a major change. First, a separate shrine had been erected on the southeast. Then, in LM IIIA2, when P was being constructed at Kommos, a series of new buildings rivaling those at Kommos were built. Apparently, they were conceived of as a group. One, a large megaron (ABCD) was probably connected with administration although it may also have served as a residence. Its plan is reminiscent of that of a mainland (Mycenaean) palace; no floor features or other remains aid in its interpretation, however. North of it were houses. To the east was a small stoa (EF) facing onto a court bordered by a portico; perhaps the two covered areas served as reception areas for the larger building. At the same time an enormous portico, a functional predecessor of the later Greek stoas, was built on the northeast, facing out onto an open area and with its columns and piers west of a series of rooms, which probably were shops, storerooms, or both. Stairs on the north reached a second story with a similar plan. Together, shrine, megaron, two stoas, and houses reflect a coherent combination of rule/administration, commerce, and social activity. Earlier, before the desertion of the Phaistos palace, the luxurious buildings at Hagia Triada may have been chiefly residences, although clay tablets inscribed with Linear A script show that produce of the area was being accounted for on behalf of the residents.

In summary, toward the end of the prehistoric period, when the Phaistos palace was largely deserted, major initiatives were undertaken at the two major nearby sites. Kommos continued to be occupied and at least two enormous ashlar buildings there, also related to storage and commerce, replaced the earlier one. At the same time or shortly afterward the regional administrative center shifted from Phaistos to Hagia Triada, and the associated commerce played a major role. It has been suggested, in this connection, that Hagia Triada now replaced Phaistos as the arbiter at Kommos, and that Kommos thus became the harbor town of Hagia Triada, itself originally a dependency of the now largely desolate Phaistos. The ancient, Minoan name of Phaistos, we deduce from tablets found at Knossos, was "pa-i-to," that of Hagia Triada or Kommos (or both) may have been the "da-wo" where, according to the tablets, immense amounts of grain were gathered even after the palaces lay in ruins.

The historical and archaeological situation of Kommos during the next thousand years or so, until not long after the birth of Christ, is very different from that during the Minoan period. Activity at the site now centered on a series of rural shrines. Since it was no longer a major settlement or harbor site—now located at Matala and Lendas to the south—Iron Age Kommos hardly participated in major historical events. This period of Greek history in Crete is not yet well known, partly because Crete was no longer the great cultural innovator and political leader it had been during the Minoan period: that role was assumed by Athens and other Greek states. As a result, archaeologists have often preferred to excavate Minoan sites, which are also usually richer in artifacts.

After Crete's capture by the Romans in 69 B.C., the Mesara flourished, later becoming united with Cyrenaica in North Africa as a Roman province. The principal settlement was at Gortyn (Fig. 63), which was an independent city-state before the Roman conquest, and typical of those in central Crete where Dorian customs of seasonal armed strife with neighboring states had replaced the apparently more pacific Minoan culture. At the time of the Roman conquest, Gortyn had seen an opportunity, in collaboration with the invader, to subjugate its

Fig. 63. Gortyn's Temple of Apollo

neighbors and rivals. The political result was that Gortyn was rewarded as early as 27 B.C. by becoming the capital of the new province. Gortyn flourished and expanded until as late as the Byzantine period. Thus the Roman city was built over the foundations of the early city-state. Even now many of the early Gortyn town buildings lie obscured until future archaeological work locates them below the thick upper level of Roman remains.

The archaeological result is that even though areas of Late Roman Gortyn (a large city with enormous buildings such as the praetorium, nymphaion, theater, and odeion) have been at least partially cleared, earlier Greek remains are few. A somewhat similar situation exists at nearby Phaistos, where the Minoan palace and some Minoan and Greek houses on the hilltop, as well as a ruined temple, have been cleared and studied, but the nearby Greek acropolis remains almost untouched. Moreover, the area of the lower towns, with Roman upon Greek upon Minoan, lies untouched deep below the present tilled fields. Hagia Triada, aside from occasional remains of a Greek sanctuary (figurines, an inscription, an altar?) was deserted during the Greek period. At Matala to the southwest the recovery of the Greek town has never been attempted, no doubt at least partly because it is deeply covered by Byzantine and Roman levels. Now it is too late, at least during this century, for Matala has become a tourist center, adding another, if tawdry, layer above the Byzantine accumulation.

The Greek remains at Kommos are confined to the flat area south of the hillslope. Perhaps surprisingly, the Greeks never built or occupied the hilltop to the north, although we know that they used, even fortified, the hilltop to the south, in connection with a small Archaic Greek settlement. When excavation was being contemplated at Kommos we did not suspect the presence of Greek remains, for the simple reason that they were covered so deeply by drifted sand blown from the mouth of the Geropotamos River—at some points the sand is over six meters deep. Thus, only Minoan pottery sherds and a few wall stubs could be seen, and those were along the western cliffside of the northern hill.

"A GREAT MINOAN TRIANGLE"

As excavation continued, it became clear that Kommos had not been just a small sleepy seaside village but, rather, a fair-sized town with large successive "civic buildings," and with connections with both Eastern and Western Mediterranean lands. The town had a significant history during the Neopalatial and later periods (we were to learn more about its earlier chapter of use—the Protopalatial period of Building AA—but only after 1991 as excavation continued on the south). In 1984, it seemed that the time had come to try to fit Kommos into a regional historical context. Also, we could present new information about how the unexpectedly large buildings being revealed might be explained. Since we wanted a public forum we chose the annual meeting of the Archaeological Institute of America, reserved a room, publicized the event, and recorded the proceedings.

The title we chose for the event was "A Great Minoan Triangle," designating the three large prehistoric Minoan sites of the western Mesara (Phaistos, Hagia Triada, and Kommos; see Fig. 64) as they might appear if straight lines were drawn between them, the base of the triangle being Phaistos and Hagia Triada which are in a rough east-west line on each end of what might be called the Phaistos-Hagia Triada ridge, with Phaistos on its eastern end. One of our English colleagues complained about the original title of the conference ("THE Great Minoan Triangle") because in north-central Crete there was another triangle (Knossos, Archanes, and Tylissos), and thus the change in title. At the meeting I moderated the presentations by our staff. Although he could not attend, we were graced by a paper submitted by Vincenzo La Rosa, director of the work at the two great archaeological sites of Hagia Triada and Phaistos. The paper outlined his novel views about the interrelationships between the two sites over time. He suggested something one could not learn from most sources, namely that the Phaistos palace was not totally rebuilt shortly after its MM II destruction, as was usually assumed. He also presented his belief that, rather than simply serving as a "summer residence" for Phaistos royalty, Hagia Triada actually played a major leadership role in the Neopalatial period. For our part, this was an opportunity to speculate about why a building as large as our T would be constructed at Kommos. It also gave Maria Shaw a chance to propose her theory that our Building P with its galleries was actually the Bronze Age Aegean version of the well-known Classical shipsheds that protected wooden ships during the winter months (see Part IV). At the same time Philip Betancourt explored the possible changing relationships between the three sites of the triangle. L. Vance Watrous discussed ceramic evidence for international trade, especially the unusual Late Bronze IIIB wares imported from as far away as Sardinia.

Looking at the western Mesara from a regional point of view, examining known centers individually but also comparing their vicissitudes, was a result of collegiality. But other factors provided opportunities. Italian excavators were in the process of re-examining through careful soundings the conclusions of their predecessors as well as their own. Another was that we had begun reconsidering the question of the relative pottery sequence. How did it compare, especially that of the First Palace or Protopalatial Period (MM IB–II), with the sequence of ceramic periods established by Evans and his predecessors in north-central Crete? How did the differing relative ceramic and archaeological sequences proposed by Italian (and other) archaeologists measure up? Until that time the sequences at Phaistos and Knossos might be compared to a similar "language" but with such differing "pronunciation" as to be only partially intelligible. Especially important for the interchange regarding relative sequencing were Italian and other archaeologists' visits to our storeroom areas where pottery could be examined, and return visits by our staff to their storeroom center at Phaistos.

One of the results of this interchange between our two archaeological groups, where the chief language of discourse is appropriately Greek (rather than Italian or English), has been a recent constructive refinement by Aleydis Van de Moortel of the MM III–LM I ceramic chronology of the Mesara. Perhaps more important is an extensive chart to be published in *Kommos* V, some twenty years after the "Minoan Triangle" conference was held, a mutual effort by members of the two groups outlining the extent of settlement at all main known sites in the western Mesara during the Bronze Age (ca. 3000–1000 B.C.). This charting is made possible by the relative chronology of the pottery associated with the remains, which indicate when those settlements were inhabited, which in turn allows us to attempt to relate those individual sites to each other. Thus the dynamics of relative growth and decline can now be investigated for various periods over some eigh-

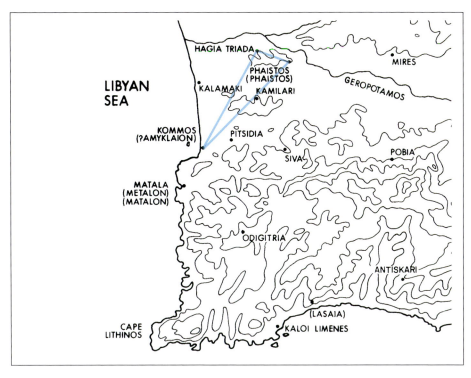

Fig. 64. "A Great Minoan Triangle" (detail of Fig. 46)

teen hundred years of history as a result of a collaborative effort by archaeologists working together to recover the history of a large complex area by means of survey, excavation, and study. In the future, new sites, changes in relative chronology, and new ideas can be added to this base.

PART III. THIRTY YEARS OF DIGGING

Fig. 65. Work within Minoan House X during 1991

Excavating on the same site for thirty years, as we did, was a long journey; one year sometimes melded almost seamlessly into another. When I think about some of the great moments we had, I realize how instrumental those experiences were in keeping us coming back year after year.

A few of those moments served as aperitifs to what followed. For instance, one thinks back to the early pre-dawn mornings as we went out to the site, after breakfast in Pitsidia where we had rented rooms for storage, conservation, cataloguing, cooking, and sleeping for a crew of some twenty supervisors, technicians, and students. Almost half of us piled into a large International Harvester van while someone went down to flag us onto the main road which was so elevated as to be dangerous for anyone approaching from the side as we were. We drove slowly in the dark for about two kilometers, stopping as we came to a turn into a rough side road—there half the crew descended, preferring to head down toward the sea along that path leading down through sand which became deeper as one approached the shore in the pre-dawn light.

The rest continued on to the small church of Hagios Pandeleimon where we stopped on a precipitous hill next to the sea (see Fig. 1, right foreground). Down we went, carrying our equipment, following the steep path leading north, first winding around a deep cut in the hillside where toward the end of World War II the Nazis had installed artillery intended to interfere with any invasion of southern Crete from North Africa, an invasion that never came. Then, before us, the shore opened up as we came down to the level of the beach but still high enough to see the hill of Kommos before us with workmen, some on donkeys or mules, silently approaching. And to hear the constant sighing of the nearby surf as it first explored the shore, then retreated. Our own slogging through the sand was audible, too, but still the surrounding quiet remained dominant as we passed by tamarisk trees that appeared as if stationed along the way. Another day was about to dawn, and it was cool, cool enough for a jacket. That would all change as the sun rose so that by mid-day we sought the relief of shade and welcomed an occasional breeze from the sea. The heat was felt by all as digging continued, whether by the pickmen who led the work teams or the supervisors who tried to maintain the recovery order of the features and items discovered, and describe them with care and accuracy in their precious notebooks. But it was those early morning walks toward the site, before access roads were built over the sand, that blessed the days that were to follow.

After the first season of excavation, described elsewhere here, we knew that we had discovered a worthy Minoan town that lay covered within an earth level that was in turn buried below a layer of sand which, on the north, was a foot deep but became deeper the farther south one went. That was in the early fall of 1976. In 1977, therefore, we set about beginning to clear the sand off the hillside (see Fig. 2), a project that continued until the 1990s as land purchase and excavation extended southward.

In the first stages of that process I consulted a bulldozer operator about how to clear the sand—don't use a bulldozer, he said, it would destroy anything in its path. Rather, hire front loaders with a great flexible scoop up front and a good operator. We fortunately took the latter path. A few of us came to Crete in May to supervise sand clearing, an operation that began on the top of the hill and continued south. Sand was dumped over the sea cliff on the west, and then the machine went back for more. Week after week, hour after hour, from early morning until quitting time in the mid-afternoon the work went on. Slowly the site was cleared of sand and brush until, aside from the trees that were trimmed but otherwise undisturbed, it was white and bare.

One surprise during the sand clearing was that while on the hillside the upper surface of sand sloped slowly down toward the sea to the west, the earth surface (which covers the houses of the Minoan town) sloped to the east. There was a hidden landscape. Thus the sand became as deep as two or three meters as we cleared downhill and eastward. This reflected a similar slope in the underlying bedrock and, when we came to excavate here later, we would dig down within ancient Minoan buildings still standing over two meters high.

Another, not so welcome, surprise came as we began to clear sand—bits of rusted metal and the calcined tops of ancient walls appeared near the edge of the western cliff above the sea, where after World War II Allied soldiers had gathered anti-tank mines laid to prevent amphibious landings and had detonated them—pieces can still be seen scattered along the shore, not only where we excavated but for at least a kilometer to the north. Most of the mines had been gathered up, but we still found pieces of them in the deep sand as we progressed to the south. One day as my foreman and great friend George Beladakis and I sat watching the front loader do its work, an entire mine a foot and a half in diameter appeared from under the tires of the front loader which had perhaps gone over it as it trundled down the hill with its scoop filled with sand. If the driver saw that mine when he returned with his machine he would surely quit and go home, never to return to the Kommos site. So instinct prevailed over caution and I ran over, bent down in the waves of sand, and picked up the heavy mine, carrying it with beating heart over toward the cliff side where I hid it, gently, under a bush. The driver never learned—I still see him in Pitsidia. The detonator in the mine, clearly enough, was rusted and immobilized after over thirty years in the sand. Word of the discovery still spread, however, and a local "fisherman" who carried out his work with dynamite, came a day or so later and removed at his peril the explosive charge, still intact, for his craft. He, as things turned out, survived to die a natural death. Someone not as fortunate, however, was one day throwing dynamite charges into the water near one of the seaside hills south of Kommos but still within sight of the excavation. The "correct" fishing method apparently requires that the charge explodes underwater, but the final blast that morning was in the air, with a spiral of smoke reaching upward. Later he was found, his arm blown off, collapsed in the shallows. He followed many who had dared deal with the explosive mines, shells, hand grenades, and the like left by the Nazis when, retreating, they abandoned Crete in 1944.

The sand clearing was always monitored that year, either by John McEnroe, a graduate student at the University of Toronto who was later to contribute important studies of Minoan architecture, or myself. The operator, George Manisoudakis, was to notify us of anything odd. One day he pointed out, under his machine, a large blue boulder in the sand—his front wheels had just gone over it. What to do? Remove it? No, we thought, so he carried out what seemed to be the impossible maneuver of lowering his front scoop down so far that the front wheels of his huge machine went up in the air, and it rested on the scoop and his two back tires. Then he reversed the machine so that the front tires passed over the boulder in question. He was then free of the impediment and could continue. Not long after he signaled again—there was something else solid in the sand. Another mine? We certainly hoped not. I poked in the sand with a shovel; it was certainly a stone. I had the driver bring his machine close where he could begin to clear near the obstruction, a process that continued for a while until, much to our amazement, a great portion of the by then two-meter-high scarp collapsed and there before us was a solid, obviously ancient wall buried deep in the sand.

Excited but perplexed, we considered such a wall. Could it be post-Minoan? All Minoan walls we had seen so far were buried in the earthen level that lay below the sand. We continued clearing, someone with a shovel working in tandem with the driver and his machine to slowly clear along the wall, which was built on the earth level. We then saw that the wall actually continued to the bluish boulder. Not only that, but we soon saw that the boulder sat on the end of the wall, then became its corner, then the corner became part of a rectangular building that was gradually cleared and, from the pottery, terracotta lamps, and roof tiles found in and around it, it was revealed as definitely a building of the Greco-Roman period, a time period not represented by the sherds we had seen along the more exposed western edge of the site. How odd this all seemed!

During the ensuing excavation season when our complement of supervisory students and workmen was full, sand clearing continued. Another building, a burned one with what appeared to be a bench around its interior, appeared on the west. In the meantime we had created a three-meter-high scarp of sand on the south, as the intervening sand was gradually carried away by a combination of work involving front loader and wheelbarrow. It was hot, demanding work done without shade. When I saw workman George, our night guard, obviously relaxing in one of the few shadows, he was soon put to work as a punishment cleaning sand from the lower part of the scarp where a few stones had been noticed. Shortly, and much to our surprise, George shouted that he had discovered some kind of strange beast and, surely he had, for there, with its head projecting enough out of the sand to be recognized, was a terracotta figurine of a bull about a foot long. There was much excitement as photographers and staff milled about recording the moment as well as the hero of the hour, George the guard. As things developed, actually, the bull was found to be standing on top of a rectangular platform (see Fig. 42) covered with the burned bones of sheep and goats—surely an altar, we thought, and odd. Had we perhaps discovered a Greek sanctuary? In the sand west of the presumed altar we knew there was another building; could it be a temple? Temples often had altars east of them. Unfortunately, we couldn't investigate, for the property didn't belong to us; we closed the excavation that year with a combination of anticipation and disappointment.

If we could raise funds for another purchase of land to the south, we might be able to acquire the property. But to expropriate via the courts the new section would (as it had with the first) take years. A cash purchase, on the other hand, might be difficult, for the first land acquisition was through an expropriation that ruined the owner's carefully developed plans to establish a hotel complex on the Kommos site. He would surely refuse to deal with us and block efforts whenever he could, nor could he be blamed for doing so.

So it was with real apprehension that in the spring of 1978 I, accompanied by lawyer Harry Bikakis of the American School of Classical Studies, traveled from Athens down to its harbor town of Piraeus, to make a purchase proposal to owner Manolis Daskalakis, who worked for the harbor commission there. I was prepared to offer a better price than the official one set for the expropriation, an inducement, if not exactly a bribe. We entered the office, were welcomed, sat down, and I described our situation. I remember a pause, and then Daskalakis said, in effect, "Professor Shaw. Your work has deprived me and my children of a considerable investment, and I resent that. On the other hand I believe in archaeology and the study of history and will let you carry out the transaction." I recall surprise, then admiration and tears of relief in my eyes as I left the building. Many years later, in 2003, I retold the story to an employee of one of the large ferry services that plies back and forth from Crete. He knew Daskalakis and told me that in the past he had heard the same story from Daskalakis himself. What an amazing act of generosity.

So the land was purchased and we cleared west of the altar with the terracotta bull and, indeed, there was a Greek temple (see Figs. 39, 41) with an interior hearth and a base at the back for at least one cult statue. The clearing was carried out under the immediate supervision of Douglas Orr, a graduate student at the

University of Toronto. The building was full of small clay lamps, pottery, partially preserved inscriptions, bronze jewelry, sculpture, and the like. Two columns had once been set on axis to support the heavy tiled roof. Three more altars, in the meantime, were found set out in the court, along with the one already described. But that is a story to be told elsewhere, and was recounted partially in *The New York Times*.

Two more great moments transpired from the discovery of that temple. One occurred after the temple interior had been carefully cleared. Its slab-paved floor was smooth from the ancient feet that had once passed over it. We could date the final use of the temple to the first or second century after Christ on the basis of the lamps and pottery found in it, but when was the building constructed? Best, we thought, to remove some floor slabs and excavate below them to recover pottery that would predate the building. This we did in the summer of 1979. First our multitalented excavation architect, Giuliana Bianco, recorded the positions of the slabs, and then they and their underpinning of stone chips were removed, right up to the last, western column base that projected down below floor level. Then, much to our surprise, we found the tops of three vertical slabs; the column base rested partially on one of them. As cleaning went on, a workman passed up a curious object—a face! A faience face! More clearing followed, and a six-inch-long faience statuette (see Fig. 37) was brought up from between the two vertical slabs found earlier. We knew once the two faience fragments fitted together that we had discovered an Egyptianizing, if not an actual Egyptian, figurine—Sekhmet, the goddess of war, as it turned out. Then one of our best workmen, Iannis Fasoulakis, announced that he had found a "hook." Again we peered into the small sounding and there was indeed a hooked metal object of some kind, wedged between two pillars. It was a bronze horse figurine (see Figs. 36, 66)! Chaos reigned. Workmen came running down the hillside to see; staff circled around.

Obviously we had discovered something special and, as yet, of unknown significance. James Wright, then a graduate student at Bryn Mawr College, spent the night in the temple until we could continue the next day, protecting the discovery. In the days that followed we enlarged the sounding to reveal that Sekhmet and the horse had been wedged between the southern two of three stone pillars. The pillars themselves, socketed into a large block, were apparently part of a

Fig. 66. The bronze horse after its recovery, with Giuliana Bianco (left) and Maria Shaw

shrine around which we found many dedicatory objects of bronze, including a number of bull figurines. There was also bronze jewelry, a few bits of gold, iron spears and arrowheads, and much decorated pottery. Upon further study the curious pillars appeared to be patterned after a Phoenician tradition of Tripillar Shrines, a probability reinforced by the discovery of Phoenician pottery from within the same context. As excavation continued in 1980 the shrine turned out to be the unique centerpiece of a temple constructed around 800 B.C. and in use for perhaps two hundred years, upon which the temple we had already cleared was located. What has come to be called the "Phoenician Tripillar Shrine" (see Figs. 31, 33) is now covered below the replaced slabs that had been removed. It will remain there, although a facsimile could be created. It serves as one of the few tangible remains, dating as early as 800 B.C., of the early westward movement of the Phoenicians as they moved past Cyprus, then Crete and Southern Italy, then south to Tunisia in North Africa, and on to Spain.

    A second revelation was brought about by the discovery of the Greek temple. While we had excavated its western end, the constructed area seemed to continue still farther west, tantalizing us as to what lay there in the deep sand. To determine that we set the front loader to clear sand along the sloping earth scarp northwest

Fig. 67. Northwestern entrance to Minoan Building T

of the temple. The machine was often so mired in sand that workmen had to help it maneuver. It was dangerous work and the driver, George (another George!), wanted to quit but I gestured for him to continue. At about the same time the foreman's whistle signaled the morning break. We retreated into the shade of the tamarisk trees for our rest and a snack while George continued. Not long afterward there was a "thud" as the teeth of the machine hit something very large and very solid northwest of and some three meters below the level of the temple floor. That was the end of our break. We picked up shovels and slid down the sandy slope leading down from the Greek temple. Gradually we revealed a huge, cut triangular block, larger than any we had seen on the site. All that day we worked to disclose what we had found. First, the block turned out to belong to a wall at least a meter thick; then as we cleared alongside it the wall itself grew in height and length to something equaling in scale the grander Cretan structures that we knew, for instance the Greek Temple of Apollo at Gortyn (Fig. 63), that great Roman provincial capital some seven miles from Kommos.

As time went on more of the new structure (Fig. 67) was cleared. We could see that it was rectangular and partly eroded along its west side by the sea. Part of its floor was preserved in the sloping scarp. We began to excavate that slope in horizontal layers so as to come down to that level. Obviously, we assumed this was a Greek structure set just west of the temple, perhaps a stoa facing the sea, an inspired siting given the setting. But then, excavator Lucia Nixon, a University of Toronto graduate student, began to reveal sherds of prehistoric Minoan pottery on its floor. More appeared but now intact and set upon and around a huge threshold block at the southern entrance to the room. Although the truth was obvious it still took time to realize that the building was Minoan, not Greek, and with blocks of these dimensions it could be designated "palatial," so similar in appearance was it to that of the nearby Minoan palace of Phaistos (see Fig. 61) or even those of Knossos, Malia, or Zakros elsewhere in Crete (see Fig. 3a). For me, this was a shock, a pleasant one but so different from my original anticipations and aims in excavation at Kommos. Having worked for years with monumental Minoan architecture at Knossos and Zakros, my aim at Kommos was to determine ways in which the common people lived and, if possible, uncover evidence of their nautical traditions and trade. Indeed, before the monumental structures began to emerge I had sketched in my imagination a simple rectangular warehouse facing the sea, not the huge set of buildings that were to be revealed in their entirety some years later (see the endpaper plan).

This large new structure, first called Building J but later Building T, Room 5, continued into the scarp and under the Greek temple we had discovered. Philip Betancourt, a ceramics expert from Temple University, insisted on its being a Minoan palace as we debated the issue during a dinnertime Canadian television network interview. As things turned out, he was more right than wrong. The very scale of the building (described in Part I) continues to amaze.

Beyond large-scale architecture, there were other substantive moments at the site. One occurred within a Minoan house called "House X" (see Fig. 65; also see the endpaper plan). House X had been discovered in 1977 after the original sand clearing operation when we dug a sounding in what was then the southeastern corner of our property. The quality of the small bronze and pottery finds suggested a special, perhaps upper-class establishment contrasting with the simpler houses already revealed on the hilltop and hillside. Later, in the early 90s, we returned to excavate House X, while also working further south of it within the larger spaces of the monumental civic buildings. The large buildings, though impressive architecturally with their fine walls and colonnaded stoas, had few

Fig. 68. Excavating the large Minoan buildings during 1993

fine small objects. House X, by contrast, was quite full of varieties of painted and imported pottery (some from Cyprus), as well as bronze tools and implements. Among the trenchmasters working at the time in the house was my wife, Maria, who with others is now completing a monograph describing the house, its contents, and its use.

Work on the larger buildings to the south was on a grander scale (Fig. 68), with many workmen and excavation teams coordinated to open large interior and exterior spaces. In House X the rooms were correspondingly smaller, the work more delicate, less dramatic and less obvious. But one day, as cleaning continued within a long and narrow space in House X, a cry of joy was heard across the southern part of the site. "A lily, a lily!" my wife Maria shouted. She and her helpers had turned over what at first appeared to be an ordinary piece of fallen wall plaster, to reveal the petals of a brilliant white Madonna lily against a yellow background, the first well-preserved Minoan fresco discovered on the site (see Fig. 15). A call went out for our conservator, then in Pitsidia, and shortly we were rewarded with a view of a fresco of a type that has made the Minoans famous for their treatment of natural phenomena. The lily, in particular, is a pictorial leitmotiv conveying this very love of nature and its abundance. Below the first fresco fragment was another, then others, one after the other. What could be more appropriate than for Maria, an expert in Minoan pictorial design, to have been the one to make the discovery. By some strange coincidence, Maria had earlier found another cache of painted plasters, this in the North Stoa of monumental Building T which had also received painted decoration, though this of an abstract character, a kind of Proto-Pompeian style of decoration imitating fancy variegated types of stone.

A different incident occurred in 1993 when we were in the process of cleaning one of the enormous galleries, almost forty meters long and six meters wide, that made up what we have called Building P (see Figs. 26, 27). As I was writing in my notebook under a tamarisk tree, Gordon Nixon, a University of Toronto student, announced that they were finding something interesting but not to come until I was told to do so. So I waited, received my summons, and soon was standing in a trench looking at two large triangular-shaped limestone slabs lying on their sides. Each was pierced by three round holes (Fig. 69), the larger hole at the apex of the triangle and the other two at each extremity of the lower part. "Anchors!" I shouted amid general excitement. Although we had found a few anchor-like pierced slabs, and naturally pierced stones before, none were so obviously manufactured as anchors. These were in a datable Late Bronze Age level (LM IIIA2) and so heavy as to be intended for use in a sea-going ship. We had now uncovered ship's equipment that expanded our nautical vocabulary and accompanied the imported pottery from Cyprus, Syria, Sardinia, and elsewhere that we had been recovering over the years. The excavation vehicle went back to Pitsidia with the news and brought the cataloguing and conservation staff. On the site, Chief Cataloguer Niki Holmes Kantzios, of Bryn Mawr College, began a dance circling the anchors, and we all joined in. Our first "anchor dance." Our workmen tolerated our madness.

Both anchors had been reused as bases within the gallery of Building P. One of them was cracked and we found a geologist to give us a proper description of the stone. He suggested that there might be microfossils (nanofossils) in the stone that could suggest where the anchors might have been quarried. A memorable correspondence between Toronto, Woods Hole Oceanographic Institution in Massachusetts, and Germany began. The result of the investigation was of great interest, for we were told that the microfossils in the anchor did not occur

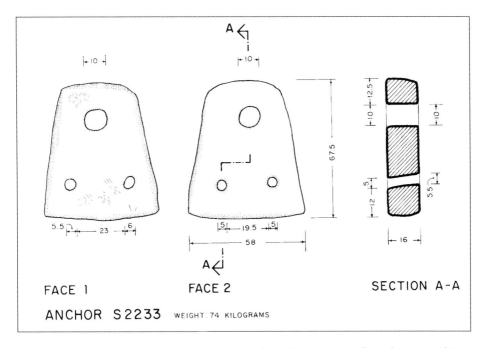

Fig. 69. Late Minoan III triangular stone anchor brought to Kommos from the region of Ras Shamra in Syria. The anchor rope would have been fixed to the end with the single large hole; sharpened sticks projecting from the other two holes would have held it to the bottom

in Cretan geological strata, but only on the island of Malta, on Cyprus, and along the Syrian littoral. Our search could be narrowed even further for there is no evidence that Malta was within Crete's exchange pattern at the time. Also, although "composite" anchors of the type we found are known from Cyprus and Syria, our anchors date to the fourteenth century B.C. and can thus be matched only to North Syria at the port of Ugarit (Ras Shamra); all similar anchors on Cyprus are considerably later. For the moment, therefore, the anchors are thought to be from Ugarit—a nautical reminder of East-West exchange during the Late Bronze Age. The best-preserved one has had a busy life since it was discovered, for since then it has made its debut in Herakleion, Athens, and elsewhere at numerous exhibitions on international trade interconnections.

AIMS AND METHODS

The idea of the excavation at Kommos developed during the late 1960s. The actual preparations and development of a methodology were to take place during the early 1970s. The methodology, of course, depended on the aims we adopted, and on our approach to the site. We felt that the excavation was worthwhile, yet our obligations to the site were a significant factor. We felt responsible for its future care.

At other excavations on which I had worked the chief aim was to recover architecture and cultural remains (pottery, metals, and other artifacts). There was little emphasis on scientific analysis of the area's topography and geology, or on any attempt to recreate the everyday lives of inhabitants. That approach was to change with the Minnesota Messenia Expedition under the direction of William McDonald, author of *Progress into the Past*. Members of his staff represented advances in North American anthropology, promoting a philosophy that supported more complete recovery and examination, one that would soon come to be reflected in excavation methodology in Greece. We consulted with them and invited members of their crew to participate in our planned enterprise. Our approach, as reflected in the early publications, concentrated on the site within its landscape, including geological and land use studies, as well as a major archaeological survey of the surrounding area with remains of all periods. Moreover, we concentrated in our excavation on attempting to recover and interpret the inhabitants' domestic economy as revealed not just through architecture, pottery, and other artifacts, but from studies of discarded bones, carbonized remains recovered through dry and wet sieving processes, as well as any remains of home industries including stone tools and metallurgy. This was in contrast to Sir Arthur Evans's Knossos work, which, although brilliant, focused on the material objects and cultural values of the elite. While Evans defined the Minoan culture for the world, much was ignored. Others excavating in Crete, however, anticipated the philosophies of the late 70s. One great example was Harriet Boyd (later Hawes) who excavated the town of Gournia in eastern Crete during 1901–1904 and whose 1908 publication can still serve as an introduction to Minoan everyday life in the late Middle and early Late Bronze Age.

FINANCING

When we began, we had little but hope, some inspired by meager evidence found at the site (mainly Minoan pottery) and some influenced by Evans's view of Kommos as the port of Knossos in southern Crete. There was no money, nor at the time any university connections that might have been of use. That situation gradually changed after we moved to Toronto in 1970. Our first offer of backing was from the late Douglas Tushingham, then chief archaeologist at the Royal Ontario Museum (ROM): $5,000 to begin with. He also generously arranged a helpful question/answer period that included professional staff from the museum. Some individuals then offered seed money, in particular an old acquaintance from my years at Zakros, Leon Pomerance, as well as Louise Stone, who was a member of the local Toronto Society of the Archaeological Institute of America. We were also fortunate to convince John Evans, then president of the University of Toronto, to furnish a sizeable amount of funding to get us started. The Canada Council in Ottawa was in the process of formation. We applied to it, with the enthusiastic help of Frederick Winter, who was my Chair in the History of Art Department at the University of Toronto, and were granted enough additional money for a first season, including funds to offset the purchase of land. We also attracted the backing of corporations, usually in the form of equipment, from the Polaroid Corporation and Eastman Kodak Company (for cameras and film) as well as Koeffel and Esser Company and the Staedtler Mars Company for drafting materials. The SCM Corporation was to assist us at a later point.

Once a first season established the site's viability, grants followed. The "grant season" was in the early fall, usually October, when applications had to be submitted, their results usually being announced in March. Their acceptance is based on "peer review," that is, recommendations by colleagues aware of the state of the field of Aegean Prehistory but still at "arms-length" from the work itself. The Canada Council (later, the Social Sciences and Humanities Research Council of Canada [or SSHRC]) throughout the life of the project (1974–2005) was the most substantial backer, but as we purchased more land and both excavation and publication became more expensive, we turned to a relatively new organization for help, the Institute for Aegean Prehistory, founded by Malcolm Wiener. For a time the Royal Ontario Museum continued its yearly contributions, but withdrew upon a Draconian ruling from Ottawa that cut Council support for many of the museum's personnel. With their research funding reduced, the ROM could no longer contribute to individuals such as myself who were not full-time staff and who had other avenues of support.

Over the years the University of Toronto provided facilities for Kommos work and, at intervals, money for research. University grants usually are negotiated with the Dean of Arts and Science, such as the recent substantial financial base for publishing our Volume V on the Monumental Minoan Buildings arranged by Dean Carl Amrhein (and Provost Adel Sedra). The president of the University often played a role. On one such occasion, President James Ham called to tell me that we were going to receive a substantial grant from someone unnamed. We received the money. After some sleuthing I discovered a few details about the mysterious donor and eventually found him to be the inventor of the radio telescope! Just as we were exploring the past by excavation, he was exploring the distant past of the cosmos with his invention. One could not ask for a greater compliment or source of inspiration.

Each successful grant, each donation, was a cause for celebration, especially as grant applications were usually the result of much time spent in preparation and thought. Once, however, while standing at a reception with a wine glass in one hand and a cracker in the other, I was approached by a stranger who said, "My name is So-and-So, and I'm considering giving you some money for excavation." "You must be kidding," I said, unable to believe that an utter stranger could be so direct. He did give, though, and has been consistently generous for the past decade.

Not all offers of contributions, however, were welcome. There was the instance of the well-heeled psychiatrist, for instance, who took me out to lunch. There he proposed contributing a sizable amount if we let him attend the excavation as an "observer," with the understanding that his profession would not be made known. He wanted to make a study of "group dynamics." I could only imagine how I, with my own personal concerns, would end up looking over my shoulder at times, or what might happen if certain members of the staff, already under stress from overwork, discovered the secret. I declined, and our chance for a group study was, happily, forfeited.

Over the years we have raised substantial amounts for excavation, land purchase, and publication. For a season's work today we need twice as much as we needed in the early days, and costs in Crete, especially after the switch from the Greek drachma to the Euro, are approximating those in Canada. Every year the accounting job is onerous. Originally, I had hopes that I could escape the chore when a brilliant Polish student, an actuary (or "super" accountant), Zbigniew Jarkiewicz, came to the University of Toronto to do his Ph.D. in Aegean Prehistory. He had temporarily left a plush job in Ottawa to pursue his life's interest. He was so capable intellectually that his general Ph.D. exams were the only instance I know of where the examinee was "lecturing" and the examiners (in Classics) were taking notes. In 1974 he designed the accounting system that we still use. He was to defend his dissertation in the winter of 1976–1977, after the first season at Kommos, but died of a heart attack in his office, in Ottawa, shortly after returning from Crete. We lost our accountant and I inherited his job. Worse, he had not defended his dissertation, and the powers that be refused every year to consider a posthumous Ph.D. since he couldn't attend his exam, an exam that, after many torturous years of study and writing, is usually a rubber stamp. Years later they relented when a Ph.D. student in English was, apparently, murdered in Florida. Her dissertation was, also, complete; she received the first posthumous degree, and Zbigniew received what must have been the second.

THE BEGINNING OF A DIG: SOME PERSONAL BACKGROUND

I sometimes wonder whether this effort of some thirty years happened inevitably as a result of circumstance; was it somehow ordained? "Collection"—all archaeologists assemble and study materials—might have begun at camp during summers in Maine when I collected local insects and then mounted them—the butterflies and moths on cotton under glass and beetles pinned in their rows in finely made cardboard containers. Certainly "digging" began in New Mexico when my Chicagoan parents had the inspiration to enroll me as a day laborer for a few months for a dig at a Pueblo Indian site of the thirteenth century A.D. by the Chicago Field Museum. From that experience I best remember the heat as we first slowly outlined room interiors and then began exposing their many levels, including human inhumations below the earth floors. One day a rattlesnake found a cool refuge within my shirt that I had laid on a wall. Director and Field Director were Paul Martin and John Rinaldo, respectively. I did not know it then, but looking through some of their publications in *Fieldiana* (No. 45, Higgins Flat Pueblo), one sees now that they were truly first class investigators, thorough and well informed, in their research into the cultures of the Mogollon Indians in New Mexico.

Brown University, which I attended from 1953 to 1957, initiated a lifelong interest in the Classical world. Though by no means philologically inclined, I was intrigued by the broadly humanistic approach of John Workman, by the enthusiastic teaching of Charles Alexander Robinson Jr. on Alexander the Great, the appeal of Greek sculpture, especially Archaic, that Prof. Robinson introduced me to during an individual seminar. It was Robinson who, during the summer of 1959, not long after a near fatal accident when I was working in a lumber mill in Longview, Washington, made it possible for me to attend the winter program at the American School of Classical Studies at Athens (the ASCSA). There I came to know and appreciate the friendship and professionalism of many who would become top-notch scholars in various aspects of ancient Greek and Roman culture—James Wiseman, David Mitten, Ronald Stroud, to mention only a few—and benefit from the guidance of legendary teachers such as Gene Vanderpool whose knowledge and subtle humor imbued the many field trips throughout central and southern Greece. In the spring of 1960, Oscar Broneer of the University of Chicago, who had discovered the much sought-after sanctuary of Poseidon at Isthmia, took me on as an assistant draftsman. George V. Peschke, the chief draftsman with whom I was to work, however, became ill, and so I was obliged to learn architectural surveying by whatever means—by manuals and by emulation of Peschke, Piet de Jong, and others. Drawing the plans of the caves near the Isthmia theater proved to be an exciting, demanding task, and brought me into contact with Betsy Gebhard, one of Broneer's students who was to publish the theater as her doctoral dissertation.

About that time I was drafted into the U.S. Army, but the memory of those wonderful spring months at Isthmia provided me with enough spiritual sustenance to carry me through the two years of service. After I was discharged I wanted only to return to Greece to take up archaeological/architectural surveying as a career. In order to learn drafting techniques and aspects of Greek architectural construction I became a student at the Illinois Institute of Technology, made famous by architect Ludwig Mies Van der Rohe.

The University of Chicago at the time (1962–1963) was still active in Classical Archaeology, under Robert Scranton who had replaced Broneer when he retired. Scranton was preparing an expedition to examine Kenchreai, the eastern port of Corinth on the Corinthian Gulf, and I was fortunate enough to be asked to do their architectural plans and drawings. Thus began a warm and close association with Scranton and many of his students, which lasted every summer until the late 60s.

The entry at Kenchreai in 1963 gave me the opportunity to remain in Greece during the winter. I rented a small basement apartment (with the help of Antonis Tritsis, later a successful mayor of turbulent Athens, whom I had met at the Illinois Institute of Technology) and apprenticed myself to John Travlos, architect of the American School of Classical Studies excavations in the Athenian Agora. Travlos was to teach me the basics of field recording—I still carry the sketchpad and paper arrangement that I believe he designed. He also introduced me to members of the Greek Antiquities Service in Thebes, about an hour by bus north of Athens. While there, helping to make a survey of Theban antiquities within the perimeter of the fourth-century city fortification walls, I met Nikolas Platon, then ephor in charge of the antiquities of Boeotia, as well as those on the Athenian

Acropolis. For many years, however, he had been an active excavator on Crete, as well as director of the Herakleion Archaeological Museum. He had been searching for two years for a Minoan palace at Kato Zakros, a harbor town in eastern Crete. During the previous year, 1963, he had discovered an unprecedented treasure of objects within a large building he identified as the palace. It contained, among other exotica, elephant tusks imported from Syria, and was obviously a major stop for traders. During a stifado meal with others in a steamy restaurant in Thebes he asked if I would make the palace plan. If I had known more about Crete at the time I wouldn't have even hesitated before accepting. This then began my long involvement with The Great Island.

During the same period I met, first at Ancient Corinth then at the ASCSA, Maria Coutroubaki. She was an excavator at Corinth and had entered the ASCSA as a regular student in 1962–1963. She was born (of Greek parents) and raised in Cairo, had gone to Bryn Mawr College in the United States for her M.A., and was in her second year at the ASCSA, doing research for her Ph.D. dissertation on Egyptian adaptation of Minoan iconographic patterns, especially as seen in ceiling paintings of the Egyptian Middle Kingdom. Maria was beautiful and brilliant—magna cum laude from the American University in Cairo. She wrote well (as compared to my own faltering prose); was humorous, a pleasure to be with. We were married by an archetypal Greek priest, stern, with a long flowing white beard, in February of 1965. Not long after came Alexander, then Robin, who are now grown adults with their own children for us, especially Maria, to spoil. Those years when the children were young and we were struggling were perhaps our best. As an artist, and while the children were very little, Maria did restorations for archaeologists (for Robert Scranton at Kenchreai, for Oscar Broneer at Isthmia). Her help was fundamental to the difficult negotiations for the Kommos excavation, and once the excavation began she was the trenchmaster who more than anyone else set the style for the field books and other field recording. Throughout the years she has maintained independent research in aspects of Minoan/Mycenaean wall painting and iconography while at the same time writing major chapters for the Kommos monographs.

The years 1965–1966 brought about a major change. We returned to North America where Maria completed her dissertation and received her Ph.D. degree at Bryn Mawr College, during which time she gave birth to our first child. This was also when I enrolled in the Ph.D. program at the neighboring University of Pennsylvania. Harbors were increasingly on my mind and George F. Bass's course on nautical archaeology presented a challenge. I chose the history of port establishments in the Mediterranean, focusing on those along the Nile in Egypt, and Tyre and Sidon in Palestine, Aegean harbors such as Kenchreai and Athens, and Roman establishments such as Ostia and Roman Carthage. That research was to later become a chapter in a Thames and Hudson book, *A History of Seafaring,* edited by Bass.

My interest in ancient harbors having been prompted by Kenchreai and Kato Zakros, I visited the Kommos site in the summer of 1965. I knew of it because of Arthur Evans's trip in 1924 to Crete's southern coast in order to find "Knossos' southern harbor there." In the process he discovered Kommos (he called it "Komo"). As a correspondent for the *Times* of London, he wrote about it the same year, as well as in Volume II of his great multivolume *The Palace of Minos at Knossos,* which, more than any other work, laid out the chronological, historical, and cultural parameters of Minoan culture.

Years later, when visiting Aegean archaeologist Peter Warren of Bristol University in England, we took a photocopy of the pages in Evans's diary describing his historic visit to Kommos to his half-sister, Dame Joan Evans, at her home. I recall the sloping, curving paved path leading down to her doorway, and, upon entrance, the living room lit by the reflected light from the garden outside. Then she, a renowned scholar in her own right, with fingers trembling from age, clarified a few points of Evans's almost illegible handwriting, referring to her older half-brother as "Little Arthur," and commenting, "Yes, he wrote like that."

Although he didn't excavate Kommos (he was literally in the backyard of the Italian Archaeological Mission excavations at Hagia Triada and Phaistos), he wrote confidently about evidence for a Minoan town there, including a building with rows of pithoi he called a "customs house" or *teloneion,* as well as evidence for a broad road that could be identified with that connecting Knossos with its harbor to the south (apparently he did not include Phaistos in his consideration!). As things turned out, over fifty years later when we investigated the site through excavations and survey, "the building with pithoi" became simply a house on the north hill and his "road" turned out to be a later Greek fortification wall. Still, Evans's instinct was so true that we believe that the broad, east-west long paved road we found leading inland from the shore is the one that all merchants continuing to the interior would have taken, whether on their way to Phaistos, Hagia Triada, or to Knossos. Also, the remains of imported goods, especially pottery, in the Late Bronze Age levels, are true to his prescient thoughts about an emporium at Kommos.

During the next few years I visited the Kommos area when I could. I stayed at Matala to the south, one of the two ancient harbors of Greco-Roman Gortyn, where there was a tourist peripteron and a single working kafeneion run by a grouch named Manolis who, however, occasionally made good baked beans. My chief aim was to come to know the shoreline, as well as the area for a few kilometers inland. Sherds along the scarps next to the Kommos shoreline certainly attested to Minoan presence, but the remainder of the immediate area was so covered by wind-blown sand that traces of habitation such as those apparently seen by Evans in 1924 were no longer visible. To what extent could one say that Kommos had been a population center? A way to begin was to look for competing Minoan settlements in the general area.

My "survey," all recorded in my notes, took me in wandering arcs around the countryside. When I found sherds I photographed them and left them where they were. In the process I determined that Matala, while obviously a Roman port, had not been a Minoan one since there was little or no Minoan pottery in the area, an observation that strengthened the case considerably for Kommos, to be upheld later when a formal survey led by Dick Hope Simpson of the University of Minnesota Messenia Expedition team and of Queen's University was completed. Nor, inland from Kommos in the area of the town of Pitsidia, were there significant Minoan remains, constituting another "arrow" pointing to Kommos. A few kilometers north of Kommos, at Kalamaki, there was plentiful evidence of Greco-Roman habitation, but again the Minoan was hardly dominant. (Kalamaki remains must still be investigated, however.)

NEGOTIATIONS

Originally, the excavation of the Kommos site was meant to be a collaborative effort with Stylianos Alexiou. Alexiou was the director or ephor of the Herakleion Museum, as well as the 23rd Ephorate in central Crete. He would have been a pleasure to work with. He was an avid excavator and a scholar of renown, most interested in Minoan foreign connections, and a thoroughly pleasant individual. He continues to be active. I had made some archaeological drawings for him at Amnisos in 1967. Alexiou must have visited Kommos not long afterward. Along with Zacharias Spyridakis (guard at Phaistos), he examined the pottery I had also seen. He decided that an expropriation was called for—that is, the government would claim the property because it contained antiquities. It was Alexiou who first took me to the Harbor Authority of Herakleion where the owner of the Kommos property, Manolis Daskalakis, showed us a survey of the area and plans for the hotel and bungalows to be built there in collaboration with an Italian consortium.

The expropriation process would take some time. First, however, topographical plans of the area were needed, done at both large (1:500) and smaller (1:1000) scales. This I arranged through John Bandekas of Athens, who had also done the Kenchreai survey for Robert Scranton of the University of Chicago. That having been done, the actual plot of land to be expropriated had to be shown on the plans and would require a topographer. I found a topographer and arranged to go with him from Herakleion to the site. By chance, I asked him whom he worked for, and he said "Manolis Daskalakis" of the Harbor Commission. The owner of the land to be expropriated! There was a dilemma. I needed the plan in the few days I had left before returning to Toronto but could I ask him to do the job if he might be fired? I told him about the situation and he said, to my pleasure, that it wouldn't make any difference because someone else would be asked to make the plan. We went to the site and he drew in two rectangles of land, one (A) a large one and a smaller one (B) within that same area. Both began at the same point on the north, over the brow of the seaside hill with Evans's "Customs House." Both extended some 150 meters south to just beyond the point where the hillside evened out to become shoreline. "A" extended much farther inland.

Both intentionally included part of the top, side, and lower slopes of the hillside. Eventually the smaller area "B" was chosen as the area to be expropriated, since our funds were limited and we didn't know how much the land would cost. The choice turned out to be the better one.

We were then told that the separation of official shoreline into public and private property had to be shown as well. This was to be decided by a special committee that would need to travel to Kommos. The chair of the committee was named Kapitanakos. We would pay the expenses for transportation, but could not pay anything additional lest it appear to be a bribe. On my last day in Herakleion, before leaving for Toronto, I left the requisite copies of the plan and the money on his desk with a letter in which I pleaded for the job to be done. Later, although I was chastised for having left cash, it was done, and I remain grateful.

It is said that bureaucracy moves slowly. This we had confirmed the next year when, upon inquiry, we found that the Kommos expropriation papers had not yet been completed. So Maria and I had to go and interview the responsible person in the chain of command and "help" the papers progress from one dingy office to the next. We bought coffees, laughed, photocopied each form as it was prepared and stamped. In one case, an original was lost but was replaced with one of our copies, then recopied.

In the meantime I had prepared an illustrated pamphlet about Kommos and the promise it held. Ephor Alexiou sent a copy along with his request to Athens, upon which the Director of Antiquities Spyridon Marinatos informed him that the excavation could not be a joint Greek/American enterprise because of its possible future scale, but had to be carried out independently by a foreign archaeological school. This meant that we had to compete for one of the precious "American School" permits. (The Canadian Institute of Archaeology had not yet been founded.) Alexiou, out of courtesy, showed a copy of the pamphlet to Doro Levi, then director of the Italian School of Archaeology, who generously allowed another archaeological group to work in a general area that had been explored primarily by Italians. He was to visit the Kommos site often as we progressed. "One palace is enough," he said, referring of course to his many years of work at Phaistos.

We were in what seemed like an untenable position then, without money to pay for the expropriation, without one of the precious few permits of the American School of Classical Studies, and without the land to work on. But we were patient and kept asking, arguing, trying to convince people that if we had just one of those three variables that we could manage the other two. Eventually that did happen—money became available and a one-year permit was granted with hesitation by an excavation committee that visited Kommos and decided there was nothing ancient there but that the site was "great for swimming." Only the land remained, and I learned in that early summer of 1975 that the decision on the price of the expropriated land was being set in the Chania courts. I also learned the name of one of the lawyers involved. I recall calling him from the Park Hotel in Herakleion in the late afternoon. He was in the shower but, yes, he remembered the case and the price, which came to $17,000 Canadian. We could actually pay for it! (Fortunately we had chosen the smaller area "B" as the land that the government would lay claim to.) I recall the euphoria, and the search for an acquaintance to join me for dinner. Fortunately I ran into two other archaeologists, Geraldine Gesell and Leslie Day, now famed for their return to excavate Kavousi, a Late Minoan-Early Greek site in East Crete explored early in the twentieth century by Harriet Boyd. We had a wonderful dinner at a small restaurant, now gone, near the famous Morosini Square of the Lions where the chief waiter was a kind man called Manolis. We could now begin, for excavation was no longer a dream but a reality.

THE FIRST DAYS

Excavation was to begin on the first of July. There was much to do before that time. In Athens I bought, from a disappointed permit applicant, a large International Harvester van, which someone dubbed "The Armadillo," that we were to keep over a decade. It was roomy enough for six, but we found later that in a pinch thirteen could fit into it. We loaded it with much of the equipment we would need, including buckets for pottery collection. Cots and mattresses we piled high on the roof rack. John McEnroe and I traveled to Crete aboard a ferryboat and then drove the overloaded van slowly over the mountain roads to the Mesara Plain, the largest plain in Crete. On the way we stopped in Hagia Varvara, where women, many in black, surrounded the van. They wanted to buy our mattresses, assuming that we were peddlers.

In Pitsidia (see Fig. 54), the town closest to the site, thanks to Petros Kyprakis, a helpful and intelligent local resident, we rented a partly built house with a spacious courtyard, another house where staff would sleep and eat, as well as space in a "rooms for rent" establishment on the village square, whose present owner, Fofo Spinthakis, still provides us with accommodation. Prior to the arrival of staff another Pitsidia resident went with me to Herakleion and helped me either buy or order especially strong shovels, large and small picks, and a fleet of wheelbarrows, also tags and the like for small finds and pottery. We would begin in July with nine staff and fifteen workmen; George Beladakis (Fig. 70) was our foreman, a calm and genuinely friendly person who, along with his family, was to be my close friend until his death only a few years ago. I chose him over others because of his humor and relaxed manner; he also was the only one who had previously worked on an excavation, namely at Phaistos during work on the west wing of the Middle Minoan palace under the direction of Doro Levi. George had a way with people. For instance, when a fight broke out between two burly workmen, George intervened masterfully, smiling and being kind, and antagonisms melted.

Not long after dawn on July 1st, 1976, we began digging, but not before a ceremony had been performed, for the local priest Papageorghis Sphakakis had been asked to bless our enterprise. He stood on the hilltop dressed in his formal

Fig. 70. Six Pitsidians who played a role in the excavation. Top row from left: George Beladakis, first foreman; Sifis Fasoulakis, second foreman who replaced Beladakis when he died; Nikos Spinthakis with a conical cup. Bottom row: Manolis Kadianakis; Aristotle Fasoulakis, now over 100 years old; Iannis Fasoulakis with a Greek bronze bull figurine

Fig. 71. The blessing of the site before excavation by Papageorghis Sphakakis, with workmen and other Pitsidians

robes, surrounded by all of us, including many workmen and interested townsfolk (Fig. 71). He dipped basil into a bowl of clear water, shaking it onto the sandy, brush-covered ground which we prayed would prove fruitful. Within a day there were results as we discovered ancient walls, rooms, and a benched court directly below where Papageorghis had stood while making his blessing. Making the initiation even more promising, we discovered a large, fine funnel-shaped rhyton (see Fig. 12), a vase thought to have been used with liquids on ritual occasions—a match to the priest's water and basil rite. Farther down the hill, on the slope, the team came upon a great mound of the collapsed stone walls of a substantial house. The trenchmaster was perplexed as to what stones not in their original positions should be removed. As he sat in contemplation, one of the workmen, Manolis Kadianakis (Fig. 70), still alive now at over 90 years of age, leapt into action and began removing stones helter-skelter—his way of helping out a distressed trenchmaster. Not long after, someone began to uncover the upper tip of a cup, and then more of the cup until we could see that it was set into the top of a tall, pipe-like vase with handles along its side (see Fig. 13). As the site photographer, I took numerous shots; then Phil Betancourt, a ceramics expert, pronounced it a rare "snake tube," a religious vessel of LM III date. The conical cup set into its top was perhaps an offering. While L. Vance Watrous, also a pottery expert, was sorting through the earth sieved from the area, he found two terracotta birds with their wings open, as if in flight (see Fig. 13). He fit them onto the handles of the snake tube—sacred birds on the handles of a liturgical vessel. The discovery confirmed a theory, published only a few months before in *The American Journal of Archaeology* by Geraldine Gesell, to the effect that "sometimes conical cups may have been set into the tops of snake tubes." At Kommos we had discovered living proof. Word went out and, within days, she was one of the first of our many visitors.

A third, final sounding was attempted in the far southern part of the site in the deep sand. Proper vertical scarps could not be maintained there because the sand would simply collapse, but a workman, the patient and humorous Nikos Spinthakis (Fig. 70), dug down for almost two meters until he struck a terracotta object, then another. He called for a whiskbroom, and gradually we saw with amazement that there were roof tiles spread out on the bottom of the trench. Roof tiles? The Minoans didn't use roof tiles, but the later Greeks certainly did. Therefore, despite the fact that no Greco-Roman sherds had been found anywhere else on the site, here was proof of a more recent phase of occupation, with tiles of course denoting buildings. A photo was taken just before the trench scarps collapsed with a "poof"! The tiles were thus hidden from view, not to reappear for at least two years when we were excavating the Greek Sanctuary, one of the great surprises of the Kommos excavations. What we hadn't known at the time is that our trench had come down within the Greek temple, onto the tile collapsed from its roof.

PART IV.
SOME
THOUGHTS ON
CONTRIBUTION

The church of the Evangelistria.
For detail and caption see Fig. 76

Having spent so much time on a single site—unusual for an archaeologist, who often goes from one site to another like a honey bee changing flowers—it is worth asking what we learned about the Minoans and the Greeks from the excavation. Of course, no one site is identical to another, as no one house is the same, and each pot is different, but still, from a general overview, what knowledge "of substance" can we claim? It is difficult to be definite; even for a general presentation such as this, one feels compelled to qualify statements. A talented colleague of mine, often timid about drawing historical or other conclusions, once said that what really mattered were the facts of an artifact: its size, color, weight, etc. But surely we can go beyond that to investigate some of the more interesting contexts discovered at the Kommos site, whether Bronze Age Minoan or Greek.

"THE STRANGE AND WONDERFUL"

One of our main aims at seaside Kommos, if the site turned out to be substantial, was to investigate evidence for Bronze Age maritime activities, especially commerce. Once we began excavating, the pottery being recovered turned out to be massive, much of it in the collapse or destruction levels accumulating as earth roofs and rubble walls disintegrated. In some cases pots of various sizes and types were actually found lying on the floors of the buildings where they were used. Pottery, indeed, turned out to be the most common artifact discovered and collected, by a factor of at least fifty to one. The closest rival would be architecture, which, however, is always left, aside from a block or two, where it was constructed. To accommodate such masses of pottery, after they had been cleaned, we set up as many as fifteen or twenty movable tables where sherds (the pots were usually broken) could be studied individually.

With the thought that there might be non-Cretan ceramics among all this pottery, we began a crude system for ferreting it out. It began with a simple cardboard box perhaps 5 inches by 14 inches, which was humorously labeled "The Strange and Wonderful." Into this box went sherds with odd shapes or decoration. Also any with unusual "fabrics." By fabric, we mean the composition of the clay used for the original pot. Were there numerous inclusions of small pebbles or tiny broken bits of pottery, or was the fabric thin and fine, with few inclusions? What of the color of the clay—was it peculiar, unlike what was most common and likely to be made locally? We clearly admitted from the beginning ignorance of foreign fabrics and hoped that finding "The Strange and Wonderful" was a legitimate way of at least determining what was non-Mesariot pottery.

As weeks went by the box began to receive "customers," all of them labeled as to their provenance. Some would be removed as we learned more about the variety of local wares in the area of the "Minoan Triangle." We had to consider also the wares imported from the Knossian area in north-central Crete. Nevertheless, the box began to fill. As archaeologists learned that a new site, Kommos, was being excavated, many came to visit. There was, however, an "entrance ticket," especially for those with ceramic experience abroad, namely that they first had to examine the contents of the box. In this way our first pottery from Cyprus was identified, and once the type was known we were able to identify other examples (see Fig. 52). After having excavated the early Greek temples we paid to fly in an Israeli archaeologist, Eliezer Oren, who was to examine in particular our Syro-Palestinian storage jars from Late Bronze Age contexts. When he looked through the "S and W" box, however, he came across some plain but identifiable fragments of what he claimed were Phoenician amphoras, probably from the coast of Syria. Here was an exciting suggestion, for they came from contexts related to the Tripillar Shrine. We promptly invited someone familiar with those fabrics, Patricia Bikai, who had published in 1987 *The Phoenician Pottery of Cyprus*. She confirmed the identification and noted that this is by far the earliest pottery group of its type found west of Cyprus. Her chapter in one of our volumes describes the pottery and lists the findspots inside and outside the temples.

Among the first "odd" ceramic finds from the Kommos houses, especially those on the hilltop, were lidded thirteenth-century B.C. jars of dark fabric, burnished, handmade, and thus unlike most of the other Kommos wares. They also emerged from within the "S and W" box. Their origin was eventually tracked down by L. Vance Watrous as being from Southern Italy or Sardinia (Fig. 53)—again, experts invited in confirmed this identification. These imports possibly had transported scrap bronze that was much needed in Late Bronze Age Crete and was apparently plentiful in Sardinia. Here was another maritime connection, completely unexpected, with the Western rather than, as is more normal, the Eastern Mediterranean. Of historical interest is that about the period of time that Sardinian pottery began to appear at Kommos, Eastern wares became less and less common—surely a causal connection that requires further investigation.

Experts such as Oren would often "reject" our identifications of foreign wares based on fabrics or shapes. Such was the case with the rim of what we first thought was a Canaanite storage jar, similar to others that had been identified. It was to emerge again from the "S and W" box only when it was identified as the rim of an Egyptian jar, one of the first such plain ware vessels to be identified in the Aegean. Later, this so-called rim sherd was to be re-identified not as the rim of a storage vase but, instead, as the bottom of an Egyptian stand. We began to build up groups or "families" of foreign wares and invited ceramic experts working in Egypt to examine our examples of "Egyptian" wares. They confirmed some but rejected others as being of "unknown provenance" (back to the "S and W" box).

These assembled "families" of non-Kommian wares varied over the years. For instance, a "family" first thought to be non-Cretan was later identified as being from the Pediada plain of Crete, not from abroad. Another turned out to be from the island of Gavdos, southwest of Crete. A Middle Bronze group, first labeled Cypriot by visiting Cypriot archaeologists, now appears so similar to a group from elsewhere in Crete that a non-Cretan origin could only be confirmed by new comparative petrographic analyses. Italian colleagues examining pottery from inland sites did not find the kinds of imported pottery being found by us. Why not? Our explanation is that after the pottery arrived at Kommos much of it found its way into Kommos households. It was, after all, ordinary rather than exotic and was therefore not sent inland, for instance, to Hagia Triada with its elite tastes. Concurrently, the contents of larger storage vessels, for wines or resins such as a Canaanite one from Syria-Palestine, were decanted into smaller, local jugs and sent inland. Raw materials sent inland, such as copper or bronze ingots, would often simply be consumed and might not appear in the archaeological record. One of our Italian colleagues, Enzo La Rosa, on the other hand, has suggested to me that Kommos may have been more independent of inland centers than has been thought.

The total of such imported items equals in number all of those identified elsewhere at Aegean sites. Even by itself the group forms an important body of evidence to suggest the directions of some trade routes. Also, the contexts within which the pottery was found can be used to determine specific chronological periods when traffic arriving in southern Crete seems to have been more frequent. These analyses were first utilized by Vance Watrous in one of our publications, and recently refined and expanded by Jeremy Rutter on the basis of new material excavated and/or identified since Watrous wrote. Rutter has also added a new Western Anatolian "family" to our groups. The origin of trade routes remains a mystery. For instance, does the existence of Egyptian pottery at Kommos imply that ships from Egypt came to Crete or that Minoan ships sailed the few days southeast to the Nile delta? Perhaps both, but we also know that Egypt was in close contact with Cyprus, so Cypriot ships could well have been the "bottoms" responsible for bringing Egyptian goods to our harbor town, especially non-elite goods such as we recovered.

A more vexatious question concerns the overall chronological contexts of imported pottery versus the chronological pattern established for the building and use of the successive monumental buildings AA, T, and P in the southern part of the site. If one conjectures that AA was originally designed to further international trade, for instance, ceramic evidence showing that to be true is limited, but then AA was so destroyed that little evidence for its use was recovered. A similar argument could be made in connection with Building T, especially considering that the peak time when imports were arriving at Kommos was long after T had gone out of use (in LM II–IIIA1). Jeremy Rutter suggests that the rise in overall numbers at T (from 26 to 126) is due to rulers of Knossos who were in control of south-central Crete at the time and promoted international trade to further their own interests.

For the period of Buildings N and P, the general sources of the imports are the same (Egypt, Syria-Palestine, Cyprus, Western Anatolia, Aegean islands, Mycenaean mainland), but with the addition of the aforementioned Western trade with Sardinia. The totals (141) are slightly above those from the previous period (126), and could well be connected with the presumed function of Building P as a shelter for ships during the non-sailing winter months.

"Minoan Palaces"

The term "Minoan palace" began with Evans's excavations at Knossos where he uncovered a huge structure (small when compared with some of Egypt's complexes, but still the largest Bronze Age Aegean building) consisting of exterior courts and four wings surrounding a rectangular court oriented north-south. Knossos's unusual, elegant architecture, its frescoed decoration and contents, provided the context for his interpretation of Minoan life. The Minoan (after Minos) palace of Knossos (with its royalty and elite taste and activities) then became the yardstick for measuring structures discovered later (e.g., at Malia, Kato Zakros, Petras, Galatas). There was some uniformity in the history and layout of the first of these structures (Knossos, Phaistos, Malia)—all had two main periods of use (Proto- and Neopalatial). All had areas for storage, for residence most likely, and for gatherings situated somewhere in the four wings.

As excavation has progressed, other such centers have been found, and they differ somewhat. Galatas, for instance, does not have a west or south wing, nor does it have a monumental Protopalatial predecessor. Petras, near Siteia, is tiny. Although Petras has a Protopalatial phase, that phase begins in Middle Minoan II (rather than Middle Minoan I as the "big three"). The Kommos "palace," T, also has a Protopalatial predecessor, which like that at Petras was founded in MM II. Also, while Building T had the requisite four wings (the western one has been destroyed by the sea), it seems to be missing some of the grander halls and sophisticated architectural embellishments found in other palaces. The result has been attempts to rethink or recast these civic or "community" centers. One suggestion has been to refer to them as "court-centered" buildings, but such a neutral term is unsatisfactory since it does not explain function. Indeed, a recent conference in Liège, with its 2002 publication *Monuments of Minos: Rethinking the Minoan Palaces,* was quite open to a variety of suggestions. The situation will likely become even more complex as new excavations produce changes in orientation, decoration, contents, size, architectural embellishment, and the like. It seems probable that every sizeable Minoan settlement possessed one of these buildings. Kommos's Building T, architecturally spectacular for its masonry and the size of the blocks used, is only one of a number of buildings that show how the Minoans experimented with form while maintaining common elements in their larger civic buildings (e.g., the Central Court).

TWO MONUMENTAL STOAS

As described in Part I, Building T consisted of a large rectangular central court, 28.64 m east-west by 39.10 m north-south, surrounded by four "wings." On the north and south there were colonnaded stoas facing out onto the court (see Figs. 20, 24), within which people would presumably gather. The circumstances surrounding the discovery of these two stoas, the first in 1980 and the second in 1993, were quite different and are worth relating. Sometimes the process of discovery can be as valuable as the discovery itself.

The North Stoa was discovered by mistake. It was 1980, the year after Greek Temple C had been cleared. Two University of Toronto graduate students, John McEnroe (now at Hamilton College) and Douglas Orr, were in charge of groups of workmen excavating not far from each other. John was working below the floor level of Temple C, in the difficult process of revealing Temple B. Doug, who had cleared Temple C the year before, was in charge of investigating the high dump of sand and discarded material immediately south of C. Having finished this halfway through the season, we decided that he should make a sounding below the dump into "no-man's land," an area where the contexts, whether of Iron Age or Bronze Age date, were simply unknown. He discovered a dump related to Temple B and, below it, evidence for what would later be identified as a dump from Temple A. Almost two meters below where he had begun he came across a great circular disk of stone, 0.51 m in diameter, the first large one found at the site and obviously a Minoan column base (like that in Fig. 25). It was set on a circular sub-base that, in turn, was set into hard clay bedrock. It could not at the time be connected with any other architectural remains, although there was a later, rough ashlar wall set at a somewhat higher level not far east of it. South of it was a very solid exterior pavement of bluish sea pebbles.

Not long afterwards, as site photographer, I recorded our progress for the annual review in *Hesperia*. First, some scarp and wall cleaning had to be carried out, especially the face of the rough ashlar wall. That job was assigned to Sifis Fasoulakis (see Fig. 70), who was to be promoted to foreman some years later for his diligence. Sifis began work and, in his thoroughness, did something he shouldn't have done, namely he excavated below the wall. Soon he called out, "Mr. Iosif" (my Greek nickname on the site), "I've found something strange and round." The round object was a column base, battered but otherwise just like the neat one to the west. We then knew the alignment of the building associated with the first column! Also, the second column base showed that there were at least two columns in line, with a distance between centers of 3.27 m, a daring distance between columns in an otherwise conservative Minoan architectural world. Because of the layer of blue sea pebbles south of both column bases, we guessed that the interior of the stoa must lie to the north.

At that point, with pressure on the trenchmasters to write their excavation reports and make relevant drawings, news of the stoa was acknowledged but was muted by other events of an exciting season. The next year, knowing the distance between columns and the direction of the span, we located enough of the other bases to know how long the stoa was, even though much of its interior would continue to remain hidden (then, as now) below later Minoan and Greek constructions we could not remove. We would also learn more about the position of the stoa's enormous back wall (see Fig. 17). Nevertheless, even in 1980 evidence for the structure was of such a massive scale that we could not envision it.

As a footnote to the discovery of the stoa, in 1980 politics in Greece were at a boil with Andreas Papandreiou drawing enormous crowds with his oratory, urging the closing of the American Air Force bases on Crete and elsewhere in Greece. "Exo oi vaseis!" "Out with the bases!" he shouted and thousands roared their approval. So when our workman Aristotle Papayiannakis, digging in a nearby trench, heard the exaltation at the discovery of one of the stoa's column bases, he, too, began shouting in mock seriousness, waving his arms, "Exo oi vaseis! Exo oi vaseis!" Knowing the association, all of us laughed, as they say in Greece, "with our hearts."

Our major purchase of more land to the south of the stoa in 1990 was based on the hypothesis that Building J/T as it was called then (now simply T) had a central court. We knew the northern boundary of the stoa and guessed that a two-meter length of ashlar wall to the west was the western edge of the court and once part of the western wing destroyed by the sea. The pebble composition of the court itself was clear enough, but we were unsure about the northeastern border and had no idea of the court's limit to the south: perhaps there wasn't any.

In 1992, excavations continued on the newly acquired property. First the two-meter deep accumulation of sand was removed, and then a long, narrow north-south trench was laid along the line of the south-central part of the Central Court. Evangelis Vlassakis, one of the brightest of our workmen that year, began finding a broad east-west ashlar wall. By its size and the character of its masonry it was an excellent candidate for the southern wall of Building T, the focus of the season's efforts and the reason behind the recent land purchase.

The next year we decided to excavate a series of broad trenches north of that east-west wall. We made a rare discovery, a pottery kiln (Fig. 72), a find that would tell us a great deal about local production—Aleydis Van de Moortel of the University of Tennessee published its pottery, both within it and in dumps alongside it, as a *Hesperia* Supplement in 2001. At the same time work north of the wall was continuing; we were at places only twenty to thirty centimeters above court level. As often, while I was under a tree composing my director's notebook I heard a shout of excitement, this time from near the kiln area. Once I arrived at the edge of the scarp, I saw the trenchmaster, Josée Sabourin, a graduate student at the University of Toronto, dancing with arms upraised while workmen were hurriedly brushing away the earth from a half uncovered stone. With the edge of his pick a workman traced the circular edge of the stone. A column base (that in Fig. 25)! And in its original position! Once it was clear we stretched a string to the nearest east-west wall on the east, and finding the distance to be about seven meters, guessed that if there were another base it would have been set at about half the distance.

We made an "x" on the earth and asked the pickman, George Babiniotakis from Margarikari on the slopes of Mount Ida, to make a small sounding. "But I dig only in horizontal levels," he correctly complained. "Just this once," he said in mock agreement but then, the subject of all of our attention, he acted as if he had developed a sudden back pain. "Come on, George," we teased him and, finally, he began to pick carefully at the spot and shortly, we heard the sound of his pick on stone. He took the tool and gently traced, like a master, along the curving stone edge of another column base. We all cheered. The remaining four bases were discovered, one after another, as we leap-frogged along. A new monumental Minoan stoa (see Fig. 24) was thus discovered and the Central Court at Kommos was known to be complete, intact. At that point "North" and "South"

Fig. 72. The pottery kiln, restored, set within the earlier South Stoa of Building T

stoas were christened with their present titles and the vast building, although still incomplete from the point of view of excavation, had nevertheless become consolidated in our minds. Our long journey of pursuit from the first glimpse of a monumental wall in 1979, to the discovery of the North Stoa in 1980 and that of T's eastern façade in 1991 had now come full circle. A significant addition had been made to Minoan architectural history.

THE "SHIPSHEDS"

There was a regional economic revival in the Mesara during the Late Bronze IIIA2–IIIB period, as is indicated by large civic buildings constructed at Kommos and nearby Hagia Triada. One of these at Kommos, which we have called "P" (see Figs. 26, 27), consisted of six huge parallel rooms, each about 40 meters long and 6 meters wide, facing the shoreline to the west. Their floors were of dirt; on many floors there was scattered pottery, often the remains of "short-necked amphoras" (as in Fig. 28), no doubt connected with what went on within the building.

P itself is huge, covering at least 1,500 m² of space. It is the largest known structure of its period (LM III) on Crete. A comparison of P's plan with that of comparable buildings from the Bronze Age and later periods seems to indicate that P's function must have been for storage. But storage of what?

A factor in any solution we propose is that security did not seem to play a role in P's design, for there is no evidence for safe closure on the western ends of the galleries which are open to the seaside. Nor was there a protective surrounding enclosure for the open space west of the rooms themselves. Whatever was stored there was either something that was without commercial value (but why then protect it with an expensive roof?) or perhaps something that was simply too large to carry away. Another factor to any explanation is that Building P faces the shore, being some 150 meters away from the shoreline, approximately the same distance now as then.

At the 1985 conference on "A Minoan Triangle," Maria Shaw proposed that P was an Early Bronze Age form of the *neorion*, or Greek "shipshed," but not one from which ships could be launched, but rather for their storage some distance back from the shoreline during non-sailing seasons. The form itself is well known from the Greco-Roman period, having been introduced as early as the seventh century B.C. to house the expensive wooden fighting ships of the various Greek city-states, as outlined in D. J. Blackman's contribution to *Greek Oared Ships, 900–322 B.C.* In these Classical shipsheds, each ship was housed on a roofed slipway, of which there could be many lining the periphery of a harbor, as at Athens. Each slipway was about the size of the galleries of P, and, like P, had an open seaside entrance. The main structural differences between them and P was that the

Greco-Roman buildings were set very near to, and sloping down to, the seashore, whereas P is set some distance back from the shoreline, and sloping down only slightly. But then most harborage situations were quite different, for the Greco-Roman sheds were usually set within sheltered harbor basins where wave action was not a concern. At Kommos, one arranged in such a manner would have been destroyed by winter waves.

The argument for the identification has convinced many, but proof remains to be found in order to convince skeptics. The discovery of stacks of naval gear would be a good beginning. My guess is that Building P is simply the first example discovered of an otherwise unknown type of Bronze Age structure. There have been few excavations in Crete next to ancient shores at harbor towns. With time, however, there will be more excavation, on Crete and along other contemporary Late Bronze Age shores. Similar buildings will be discovered. Only then will we learn more about their function. Kommos itself could possibly provide the solution when and if P's two southern galleries (5 and 6), still unexcavated, are investigated in the future. If, however, another Building P is found far from the shoreline, we will have to regroup and formulate another explanation for the building type. Storage will continue to be identified as its main function.

LATE MINOAN II: "INDEPENDENCE AT LAST"

During 1977, as we excavated south of a hillside house dubbed "the House with the Snake Tube," we found a series of dumps consisting of discarded material, especially pottery mingled with earth. Dumps are common on ancient sites. Created before the public collection of garbage began, these dumps are usually situated at some convenient spot outside a building. In the case of the later Greek temples at Kommos, it is clear that those cleaning up inside exited at the eastern door, turned right, and there dumped their containers of bone, broken pottery, etc.

Over the years that the house was in use, the dump level rose. When we excavated it, we "sectioned" it, so that its contents could be seen from the side. There were layers with more pottery than earth; there were burnt layers with white ash; there were varying colors of brown earth. In other words, the dump was clearly stratified. Excavated material was also collected in a "stratified" manner: all contents (bones, pottery, etc.) were kept separate and sent back to our Pitsidia study center.

The pottery was particularly interesting, for, with the earlier pottery being found last, our ceramic experts could trace the development of known pottery styles of shape and decoration beginning with Middle Minoan III, then Late Minoan IA, then Late Minoan IB, all predictable and, for us in our early days of excavation, welcome, for our findings were consistent with those elsewhere in Crete. What was unusual was the discovery above the LM IB level of a layering of what Evans had dubbed for his Knossos site LM II or "Palace Style" wares (Fig. 73). This level was definitely separate from and stratified above the earlier ware, and was, in turn, below pottery of a somewhat different, LM IIIA1 style.

LM II "style" had first been recognized at Knossos, where it was found largely outside the palace, usually scattered and unstratified. A similar situation applied when it was found elsewhere, usually in isolated examples, especially in eastern Crete, where it was recognized as a "style" but not, like Late Minoan IB with its marine motifs, as representative of a specific period. The Kommos evidence, however, where one could see in the scarp the physical beginning and end of the pottery deposit in question, suggested that a specific period of time was involved.

Fig. 73. Late Minoan II pottery from Kommos: left, a jug with reed pattern; center, a cup with flower and arch decoration; right, a goblet with papyrus and volute design (after **Kommos** *III, Figs. 20, 22, 23)*

Coincidentally, at about the same time (the late 70s) a German scholar of some note wrote a short article in the *American Journal of Archaeology* maintaining that LM II should be considered only as a style, not as a period designation. Shortly, on invitation, he arrived to examine our evidence, and upon consideration reversed his stand. This reversal, plus clear evidence from renewed excavation at the "Unexplored Mansion" at Knossos and also at Chania in western Crete, have shown that, indeed, LM II pottery, known chiefly in central Crete, represents a style but, also, a definite, but short, period of time. Our new bit of information about LM II was instrumental in finally giving it "independence at last."

"DOMESTIC ECONOMY"

As explained in Part III, one of our chief aims in pursuing excavation was to discover a Minoan settlement and attempt to recover aspects of the "domestic economy" of the people who lived there. As things turned out, we were granted that opportunity, and more besides, as the rich religious contexts of the Greek Sanctuary presented the remains of banquets and sacrifices. The consequent recovery of forms of pottery, as well as faunal remains, have added significantly to our developing understanding of sacrifice and cuisine in the ancient world.

For a sober, factual accounting of the evidence for the diet of the Bronze Age Kommians in their town, one can examine detailed statistics on fauna (chiefly the evidence for sheep, goat, pig, and cattle) and flora (carbonized remains of acorns, almonds, carobs, figs, legumes [beans], and cereals [wheat/barley]). For collateral activities there is evidence for building, carpentry and tool maintenance, metalworking, oil and wine production, jewelry production, pottery making, and religious activity. This can be accomplished for the major periods of settlement (Protopalatial, Neopalatial, LM III) or for their various sub-periods. Comparative evidence from other sites, where materials are better preserved through catastrophe or simpler circumstances of preservation, provide major additions to our general knowledge.

This evidence is available for consultation. A few examples may suffice to illustrate our areas of interest, as well as the limitations of our knowledge. For instance, I am reminded of the time when we were renting rooms and almost every afternoon a deep, grinding sound came through the wall from next door. We came to know our neighbors, and found that Theonifi Kadianaki, then perhaps sixty years old, was grinding wheat for bread with a stone mill, quite similar to the process that we were finding evidence for at the Kommos site. The "old technique," now abandoned by all but the most elderly villagers, had continued since antiquity, surviving all the changes in life style. On the site, in literally all the houses, the evidence for such activities is all-inclusive—a plethora of pounding and grinding stones, sometimes referred to as cobbles or hammer stones, but also querns and mortars, appear. Some are heavy, often difficult to study, and are set aside or discarded by many excavators as simply too much trouble to bother with.

In our case, Harriet Blitzer carried out for us the first broad typological study of the varieties and uses of such Minoan implements.

One of our first discoveries of a major stone implement was made on the hillside not long after we began digging there. On a masonry platform in the corner of a room (see Fig. 11), not far below the modern surface, was a large slab cut with a shallow circular bowl-like depression. A carved spout with an open channel projected out over the edge of the platform. Clearly (confirmed by the workmen) here was a "patitiri," or a press for use in collecting liquid that would then flow out into a collection basin, an amphora or an even larger storage vessel such as a pithos, for storage and eventual use. I imagined that it was used like those still in the villages today. Another possible use, however, for the same slab was as part of a lever press to crush and process olives for their oil—now that work is done with massive presses. Found on the floor of the same room was a broken pithos, no doubt abandoned along with the press bed when the Kommians decided to move on to another site.

In the same Minoan contexts we found a number of limestone slabs with shallow rounded depressions ranging from 0.15 to 0.20 m in diameter. Some were single, one was even triple, for instance that in Fig. 74. They were, clearly, set for use with the depression "up." One immediately thinks of the "stamnostatis" still used in the village where a water jug or stamna with a rounded bottom would be set in the hollow—one could simply tip the jug sideways in order to pour out the liquid. In the old houses in the village such slabs are often usually double, set in special niches built into exterior and interior walls. There were, however, problems in our interpretation, raising cautions in the use of such ethnographic parallels, for we did not find jugs with round bottoms, rather our jug bottoms were flat. At one point we thought we had found a solution, for on some of our jugs originally made with flat bottoms, the edges of the bottoms were rounded by wear. In the end, another proposal was put forward, namely that the rounded depressions were used as anvils or molds in metalworking activity, for which evidence was found nearby. But would the slab have survived any hammering that would inevitably be part of that activity? It would be interesting to create similar objects today and experiment with them, to see, for instance, if they would survive constant hammering.

Fig. 74. "Stamnostatis" slab with three depressions, found in the House with the Snake Tube

For both the Minoan and Greek periods there is plentiful evidence for fishing and fish consumption. There are the barbed and unbarbed bronze hooks that are occasionally preserved, also net weights (see Fig. 51). The fish were mostly small ones caught along the shore, but from a Minoan context on the hillside came a tuna fish bone, evidence that fishermen went out into deep water, probably even beyond the Paximadhia Islands that one can see from the shore, where such huge fish ran in schools. By far the most exotic fish, however, was found in Temple C, a freshwater catfish *(Clarias gariepinos)* that may have arrived at Kommos dried or as part of a salted fish delicacy from as far away as Egypt.

A puzzle of interest arose in the Greek Sanctuary, in a late-seventh-century B.C. context. Thousands of limpet shells were found outside of Temple B (see Fig. 31), counted dutifully one by one by David Reese, our faunal expert. The limpet fastens itself, rather like a barnacle, to outcrops and slabs awash along the shore, where a single shell with a slight pinnacle protects it. Limpet meat, thought by some to be a delicacy when boiled and covered with sauce, by others to be inedible, must have pleased many at Kommos, and no doubt gathering limpets from the great slabs of beach rock must have preceded many a seaside meal. The puzzle has to do with a series of curious small U-shaped, open compartments (like that in Fig. 75), formed by three slabs set on edge. At least eight of them were found

Fig. 75. One of the small enigmatic three-sided "slab stands" found outside Greek Temple B

around the temple. One was found with faint traces of burning, and there was much ash found near another. Ranging as they do from 0.10 to 0.60 m on a side, one wonders if they were covered over by a cooking lid—or were actually small hearths, open on one side, used for boiling limpets. We referred to them while excavating as "telephone booths" since they were always open on one side.

Of some interest is our evidence from the sanctuary for the eating of pigs. Ancient author Athenaeus of Naucratis in his work *The Deipnosophists,* written at the end of the second century A.D., states:

> Speaking of hogs . . . the animal is sacred among the Cretans . . .
> this creature is universally regarded with great reverence and no one . . .
> would eat of its flesh (4.685)

Yet, from the pig bones recovered, the eating of pig was particularly popular toward the end of the use of Temple B. Within Temple C's hearths, moreover, there were more pig bones than those of either sheep or goat. Oddly, however, while pig remains were plentiful inside Temples B and C, they were not found among the masses of burned bones from the sacrifices made on the exterior altars. Perhaps we have found evidence that, contrary to Athenaeus, the Cretans actually ate pig, but they just did not use it for their sacrifices, preferring sheep, goat, and cattle as shown by osteological evidence from our sanctuary.

A QUESTION OF ATTRIBUTION: GREEK TEMPLE C

The discovery of a Greek temple, in our case three built on top of one another, is an unforgettable experience not granted to many archaeologists, especially to archaeologists who, like ourselves, were searching for the remains of another, earlier era. The upper temple (Temple C, for which see Parts I and III) was discovered as we were wading deep in sand trying to make sense of where we were. A few blocks and a line of wall were found, then our workman Iannis noticed that the sand alongside the blocks was denser, moister, while that above the few blocks was dry, did not retain its form, and was shoveled up easily. As he pursued the wall, it continued in a straight line. Soon a trench was formed in the sand with a moderately damp, stable scarp along its south side. Clearing continued and it soon became evident that we were in a "robber's trench," which remained after the upper wall of a building, buried for centuries in the sand, was removed by scavengers digging from above, prying out the blocks as they followed the wall. What we were uncovering was the broader foundation for the wall itself.

We followed the foundation, clearing as we went, turning as it turned, until we had returned, after turning three times at right angles, to the point we had started, outlining in the process a great rectangle of sand. That rectangle was, we knew, the interior of a building. Along its western end there was a partly destroyed base. Its topmost block was preserved, with part of the sinking for setting in a statue—the base for a cult statue. A temple had been found.

As we slowly cleared the interior of the temple we saw that there was an upper dirt floor above the original one of slabs (see Fig. 39, left). There was much pottery, dozens of clay lamps (see Fig. 40) with signs of use, and stone temple "furniture" such as water basins on stands, probably for pilgrims to anoint themselves. A bench ran around the interior. To what deity or deities was our temple in the sand dedicated? Unfortunately the cult statue was gone. Actually, as we studied the statue base we concluded that two figures, probably of marble, had been accommodated on it. All we found of one of them was an eye, as if meant to tantalize us. We then turned over a broken stone slab sunken into the earth floor to find it carved in Late Hellenistic or Early Roman style with a depiction of the goat-footed god Pan (see Fig. 44), a god of flocks and groves. Was Pan, then, the god worshipped in the temple? A fragmentary portable altar dedicated to Poseidon, the god of the sea, was also found inside the temple.

A few weeks later, when much of the temple had been cleared, we removed deep sand from east of it; I had asked the supervisor in that area to be especially vigilant for inscriptions. Not long afterwards, flushed with excitement, bow-legged, he appeared with his arms wrapped around a good sized, heavy slab of stone. "You can't have it, you can't have it," he chortled in mock earnestness. When he turned the slab over, there indeed was an inscription carved in it, with its letters painted in red against a blue background. In abbreviated Doric Greek, which is difficult to read, it cited "procreative Zeus" and "Athena of good tidings."

So, rather than a series of dedications to a single deity, we were presented with a choice when it came to identifying the main deity or deities to whom the temple was dedicated. There was Pan, but he haunts groves not buildings, so he can probably be eliminated. Poseidon remains a possibility, but the altar his name occurs on was probably placed outside the building and the base inside accommodated two statues rather than a single figure. The best guess, therefore, remains Zeus and Athena. Moreover, when Temple C was built it was associated with two rectangular altars east of it, one perhaps reserved for each deity. With the information we have, that is as far as we can go.

THE ARTEMIS TEMPLE IN THE PLAIN

While dedications to a variety of gods found in Kommos's Temple C may prevent a sure identification of the chief deity worshipped in it, quite a different circumstance surrounds another ancient temple found a few kilometers to the north of Kommos. That temple is now no more than the masonry mound of its original deep foundations surmounted by a small Greek chapel dedicated to the Evangelistria, the bringer of good news (Fig. 76). The site is also called that of the "Old Church." From the other side of the road running alongside it down to the site of Kalamaki on the shore, we had seen a few interesting architectural blocks that surely belonged to an important public building. These were recorded during the original archaeological survey of the Kommos area begun by Richard Hope Simpson of Queen's University in 1977.

Fig. 76. The church of the Evangelistria set on the foundation of the Artemis temple near Kalamaki

A problem of identification arose, however, for although the same foundation had been reported by earlier Italian researchers (by Paribeni and Guarducci in 1908 and 1935 respectively) as belonging to the base for a temple of Artemis (Diana), a French epigrapher had suggested in 1969 that the block inscribed with the name of Artemis that had furnished the original identification had actually been brought for reuse from ancient Soulia (modern Hagia Galene) some distance up the coast. This conundrum was on my mind when on a late spring day, before excavation began, I included the Evangelistria site in our archaeological walks in the countryside.

I arrived with our foreman George Beladakis (see Fig. 70) at the so-called temple site around noon. We stopped in the shade of the church to have a simple lunch, chiefly cheese and bread and olives, plus some water. I had also brought a can of Trata brand sardines, with a small very hot red pepper thrown in—a most delicious tastemaker. After lunch we scouted around the area, looking for anything of interest, gradually widening our arcs of search until we were at least twenty-five meters from the building. I saw a few blocks, then what looked like a particularly finely carved one. And on it, to our excitement, there were letters. We turned it over to look at it more carefully and there, before us, was the solution to our puzzle, a prayer to Artemis by a Roman, a Sotios Secundus, carved on a block that could only have been at the corner of a building. We would later take impressions and study the block more carefully, but I remember thinking at the time that it was that strong red pepper and sardine oil that were responsible for the discovery. Confirmation was to come later with the republication of the journal of a Florentine gentleman, Cristoforo Buondelmonti, who in 1415 had disembarked at Matala and walked north to the area concerned where, he reported,

> I observe a large temple in the plain. I call a shepherd who, answering my entreaties, has soon explained everything, namely that on the site was built the venerable Temple of Diana [Artemis] and people marvel at the vast walls which enclose the temple.

Thus the temple can now be identified positively. For anyone visiting it, it is located on the Kamilari-Kalamaki road, at the only sharp right-hand turn leading down to the Kalamaki shoreline. While it appears at first to be quite alone in the landscape, investigation by the Greek Antiquities Service, as well as our archaeological survey, suggests that the temple was on a slight height within or next to a substantial Hellenistic-Roman settlement. Unlike the Kommos temples, therefore, the Artemis temple was in an urban setting. Excavation around the temple platform would certainly be a worthwhile enterprise.

CRETAN TEMPLES UPDATED—THE "DREROS" TYPE

When I was a Ph.D. student in Classical Archaeology at the University of Pennsylvania in 1967, Rodney Young's course in Greek Architecture featured the mid-eighth-century B.C. Cretan Temple of Apollo at Dreros as an early example, if not a progenitor, for Greek temple design. I was assigned a seminar presentation on the building, which I had never seen, in a part of Crete I had only passed through. I enjoyed the experience but Young complained that I brought up too many details. I could not have imagined then that only a little over a decade later I would have the privilege to assist in the discovery of another Cretan temple in the same architectural tradition.

The Dreros Temple (Fig. 77), excavated by Greek archaeologist Spyridon Marinatos in the 1930s, was found when investigating the discovery of three very significant bronze statues in an early Greek town high in the hills of north-central Crete. Marinatos's investigation revealed a rectangular building with two wooden columns and a hearth between them, on axis. Presumably the three bronze statues, now displayed prominently in the Herakleion Archaeological Museum, were set on a platform near the middle of the far end of the building. A partial bench ran around the interior. On the basis of an inscription mentioning a temple to Apollo at Dreros, the bronze male figure was identified as Apollo and the two female figures were, accordingly, Artemis (his sister) and Leto (her daughter).

If the reader recalls our fourth-century B.C. Temple C at Kommos (Figs. 39, 41, 76) it has essentially the same rectangular ground plan with a rectangular hearth at its center, between two stone columns on axis, and a base for statues at the center of the back wall. A bench for celebrants to sit and/or lie on, as in a Greek symposium, runs around the interior of the room. The general parallel with the Dreros Temple is unmistakable, though some details differ.

In a little-known spot in southeast Crete, one finds another temple, that of Asklepios at Lissos (Fig. 77), excavated by Nikolas Platon and still unpublished. Again, the temple came to the attention of archaeologists when excellent sculpture, this time of marble, was discovered near where it had been set originally, behind a kind of low partition within the building. The plan in the case of this Late Hellenistic (first century B.C.?) or Early Roman temple is familiar—rectangular, with a possible bench on the interior, and a base for the statue of Asklepios on

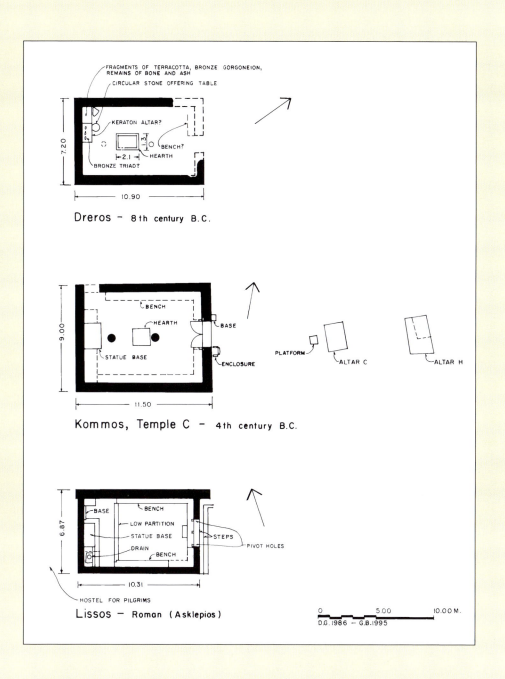

Fig. 77. The Geometric Dreros Temple of Apollo, Kommos Temple C, and the Late Hellenistic Temple of Asklepios at Lissos

axis near the back wall. The hearth/interior column arrangement found at Dreros and Kommos is absent. A mosaic, rather than a hearth, was found in the middle of the room. The columns may have been there at one time but were eliminated when better Hellenistic building techniques made them unnecessary. Like most temples, this one faces east. My guess is that it faced an exterior altar, similar to Altar C at Kommos, that still lies unexcavated below accumulated earth debris.

Ancient artifacts can often be separated into "families." We do that with pottery, which has numerous shapes and decorations, many of which can be pinpointed chronologically. It can also be done with loomweights, those clay suspension weights used by ancient weavers. So, too, with buildings such as temples, which have varying plans or "footprints," and varying interior features. In the case of Bronze Age Building P (see Fig. 27), it at this time stands as a lone example, but I suggest that it, as once with the Minoan "palace," represents a type of structure that will appear elsewhere along the shores. Three main types of Cretan temples are recognized: those with a square plan, those that are long and rectangular with a number of communicating rooms set on axis, such as the important Temple at Prinias (see Fig. 3b), and the third, a single rectangular room (or "oikos") type, now recognizable at Dreros (ca. 750 B.C.), Kommos Temple C (ca. 375 B.C.), and Lissos (ca. 100 B.C.–A.D. 100) (see Fig. 77). There is little doubt that their shared form is related, with a conservative religious tradition maintaining their proportions as well as the use of the interiors for banqueting (as indicated by the benches). An analogy with Orthodox Church architecture (the apse, the aisles, the positioning of the altars) would be apposite here.

Sometimes it takes the discovery of a link in a chain to make possible the viewing of the chain itself, as in the case of Kommos Temple C. Of course we are still unsure about the missing links, such as earlier arrangements that led to the Dreros Temple plan, or intermediate examples, still undiscovered, that led to the plan of Temple C at Kommos. Nevertheless the "families" are beginning to form, as opposed to our simply having many individual examples, which suggests progress in our understanding of this particular aspect of the past.

THE "PHOENICIAN" SHRINE AND RECOGNITION

The circumstances of the discovery of the Phoenician Shrine (see Fig. 33) have been recounted more fully in Part III. Briefly, a small, three-pillared structure surrounded by dedications of various kinds was discovered below the floor of Temple C. Further excavation established that this shrine was actually set on axis toward the middle of an earlier temple, "Temple B," around 800 B.C. These "facts" took a few years to realize, leading to a gradual recognition of what we had discovered.

Between the southernmost two of the three pillars we found a faience figurine. In order to remove it, wedged as it was, we poured water into the hole we had created and then slid it out from the muddy mixture. The head, found earlier, was then joined. A goddess, we thought, with the Egyptian ankh staff, accompanied by a cat. One of our staff, Robert Koehl, knowledgeable about things Eastern, suggested Sekhmet (see Fig. 37), a label that has since stayed with the figurine. The late Nick Millet of the Royal Ontario Museum, whom we consulted later, confirmed that it was genuine Egyptian rather than a copy. With the assumption that if there was a figurine between the two southernmost pillars there might be another between the two northernmost ones, we removed the two southernmost pillars completely (they were socketed into a large block but could be pried up with care) to find, to our delight, a smaller but no less significant faience figure, perhaps of Sekhmet's child, Nefertum. Missing was only Ptah, the husband of Sekhmet and the third of a triad representing the area of Thebes in Egypt. It seemed apparent that it was not by coincidence that the Theban triad was represented as a part of the display accompanying the Tripillar Shrine.

Sekhmet had been wedged in above a very solid, beautifully made horse of bronze (see Fig. 36). The combination of the two, exotic Sekhmet and pragmatic horse, presents a strong coupling. Sekhmet, a rare import from a fabled land, probably represented to the dedicator the power and mystery of the East, especially Egypt, to which Cretans were slowly being exposed as their otherwise isolated culture was becoming engaged commercially in this era of what some have called Orientalization. (During the same period, the seventh century B.C., Athens and Corinth on the Greek mainland were exporting their own decorated wares, which were also found as part of the dedicatory deposit around the Tripillar

Shrine.) The horse, on the other hand, represented a pragmatic part of Cretan life, in this case the accoutrement of the Cretan aristocratic elite, landowners, horsemen, and warriors often represented in Cretan art. Among the dedicatory objects, as if accompanying it, were other horses of terracotta, a bronze horse bit, and a spearhead. Moreover, a large bronze warrior's shield was found wedged in behind the three pillars, and an incised black glazed bowl depicts what appears to be an armed warrior paying his respects to another, apparently a corpse, lying on a bier covered by a patterned cloth.

During a conference on interchange in the Eastern Mediterranean, I discussed the Tripillar Shrine and our reasons for believing that it was Phoenician in origin: parallels to it in later Punic art, especially on stelae, an early tapering pillar from Cyprus inscribed with Phoenician script, plus Phoenician pottery finds connected with the shrine. Moreover, recent discoveries of Phoenician-related finds (pottery, pillars, metalwork) had recently been reported at Knossos and Eleutherna. One participant, however, questioned whether a tripillar structure of Phoenician inspiration could have been accepted by Cretans as the centerpiece for worship in a temple such as the one at Kommos. In retrospect I might have brought up the presence of Sekhmet which, although later than the Tripillar Shrine itself, represented the Oriental, the exotic, a reference suggested by the pillars themselves.

I might also have brought up the known Cretan familiarity with the idea of a Trinity, such as the bronze figures of Apollo, Artemis, and Leto found on a platform in the Geometric Temple at Dreros. "Trinities," psychologically comfortable groups of three deities, are also found in Egyptian iconography. Later, Christian dogma defined its own concept of the Trinity. My argument to her now would be that the presence of familiar aspects from an otherwise "different" iconography suggests that acceptance and adaptation were possible. After all, the influence of the East upon an impressionable Greece was profound, whether we are referring to the adaptation of the Northern Syrian alphabet or the stance and monumental proportions of Egyptian figurines. Another consideration is that Kommos with its temple was a convenient stopping off point for Phoenicians on their way west. Boeotian traders from the Greek mainland also stopped there, and inscribed on black glazed cups their names in the recently adopted Phoenician script.

"WRAPPING UP": A CONCLUSION

So far in this part of the book we have explored areas where excavation at Kommos has contributed to our knowledge of Greek culture and history. For the prehistoric Minoan period, the unusual amount of everyday pottery imported from outside Crete provides precious insights into the degree of exchange, as well as to the sources of material, and thus the directions of trade. Also, the monumental court-centered structure (Building T), with its graceful stoas, demonstrates how such buildings must have fulfilled Minoan "cultural expectations" within settled urban environments. T's successor, Building P, the probable "shipsheds," not only adds an unusual building form to our Minoan architectural vocabulary, but also suggests a new sophistication for Aegean nautical enterprise. Concurrent advances are being made in understanding the daily life of the Kommos inhabitants through analysis of their metal and stone implements, the bones left over from their meals, the shapes and decoration of their often-elegant ceramic vessels.

For the Greek period with its rural sanctuary we have been blessed to discover, essentially intact, a series of superposed temples with the remains of offerings and sacrifices left from more than a thousand years of continuous use. We are thus in an unusual position to discuss evidence for continuity and change in Greek ritual practice. And at the same time Cretan architectural traditions can be traced with more certainty than before: a "family" of temples can be identified. Of particular interest is the Phoenician-inspired shrine within Temple B, unique among Cretan discoveries but nevertheless resonant of traditions that must have been already present on the island.

As an attempt to "wrap up" our perceptions of the excavated site, we will position ourselves at two points in the Kommian landscape. First, we invite you to a panoramic vista on the modern road just east of the fenced site. From there we have a full view to the west of the southern part of the site, with its huge Minoan civic buildings and the Greek Sanctuary perched atop them, as seen in Fig. 2. The houses of the Minoan town continue up the hill to our right.

When excavation began in 1976, there was a gentle sandy slope from the road down to the seashore. There was a similar slope in ancient times, but since that time the accumulation of earth and, especially, wind-blown sand became over ten meters thick. We removed, with great care, this blanket of overburden in order to reach the ancient levels. Now, we look down into the deep bowl of the excavation, supported in front of us by enormous modern retaining walls.

Some distance from the ancient remains, we are enclosed within the sandy landscape of trees and low hills around us, free to wonder about what we are looking at and what the archaeologists, in their enthusiasm, have done. Given the geological possibility, although very long-term, that some of the site might be re-covered by sand, we can reflect that it would thus be preserved, just as it was preserved for us to find. With that in mind, there is the satisfaction that, since the detailed publication of everything we see is either well along or complete, the record will remain available for the foreseeable future. Data in those publications are "beyond summation," that is, data that can be mined in the future by historically minded professionals, such as the studies of the fauna or pottery, or the architecture.

There are immediate and temporal satisfactions as well. One can wander within a great palatial court and imagine the seasonal celebrations; the town's byways and streets invite us to visit the houses, which we can enter and where, in our imaginations, we can make ourselves at home, wonder what is for dinner. We can peer over the cliffside down to the wave-rimmed shore, or contemplate the Paximadhia Islands gray in the distance. Or one can position oneself where the priests stood in the Greek period, between temple and altar where the sacrificed lamb and goat limbs were once burning, the fragrance wafting up to the waiting gods, and hear the flute music of those in the procession, while the constant waves provide their own rhythms on the shore beyond. And one can imagine what lies still unexcavated in the two southern "shipsheds"—nautical gear, or something completely unexpected and exciting. In these palimpsests of time, with Minoan on Minoan, Greek on Minoan, then Greek on Greek, there remain mysteries, spirits, the still unexplained. We are made aware of the inhabitant's startling creations here even though their presence was transitory, once urban and active, then given over to ritual, then deserted as now.

The second viewpoint you are invited to is a few kilometers south of the site, on the edge of the rough limestone cliffs facing the north-south strip of shoreline. One reaches it by taking a side road to the west about halfway between Pitsidia and Matala. There are restaurants along the cliff edge and an ethereal view, the rolling sandy hills of the Mesara Plain shading beyond into the grays and blues of the foothills of the Idaian Mountains sacred to Zeus (Fig. 1). Crows careen here, suspended in the updrafts. On the highest of the foothills are white dots, churches erected by the faithful, no doubt as part of a vow, just like the church of Saint Pandeleimon not far from us in the foreground. It is more a part of the visible landscape than the Kommos site is, now hidden by wave-like sandy mounds sparsely covered by tamarisk (*almiriki*) and juniper (*kedros*) trees.

This patchwork of low hills before us is sparsely settled, proclaimed an archaeological zone. Otherwise the usual hotels would be lined up along the shore and the summer cottages would crowd behind them for many yards. So the excavation "saved," in a way, one of the few unspoiled shoreline landscapes in Crete. The excavation brought about another, major result, namely that now, whenever historians consider the dynamics of Bronze Age history in all of central Crete, two great Minoan sites in the area (Phaistos and Hagia Triada) are combined by historians with a third, Kommos, which provided those two inland sites with access to the sea.

To our left is the Libyan Sea over which ships from Mycenaean Greece and Cyprus and probably Egypt sailed. Later came Phoenicians, Greeks, Romans, Byzantines, and Venetians, some landing within our current view. This eternal, yet changing, landscape seems to make complex things simple, clear, meaningful. It can serve us, as we consider the complexity of what lies before us, in Robert Frost's words, as a "momentary stay against confusion."

APPENDIX: THE WRITTEN WORD AND THE DIGITAL DAWN

Evans's masterful volumes reporting on the excavations carried out after 1900 in and around what he called "The Palace of Minos at Knossos" are, at their best, fascinating interpretations of remains from the palace area and their place in Minoan culture and aesthetics. At their worst they are meandering investigations of architecture, of style and its chronology in Crete from the perspective of what was known of other Mediterranean cultures at the time. Often he becomes so digressive that the reader feels lost—one misses an orderly presentation of material and, only then, its interpretation. Fortunately Evans's half-sister, Dame Joan Evans, a brilliant scholar in her own right, put together, out of pity for the readers, the final "volume" for *The Palace of Minos* when she provided an index for it.

Surely Evans's creative approach to reporting was not the prototype to emulate. One wants more synthetic approaches to particular areas of excavation and more details about what was actually found and where. He did not provide elevations beyond a stated benchmark and, with his hired excavator Duncan McKenzie, only measured down from an irregular ground level in each area. His approach has spawned a massive body of literature attempting to associate areas and their finds, whether discussing the findspots and contexts of the inscribed clay tablets he discovered in the palace or the range of pottery, frescos, and other objects from the many houses and structures outside the palace borders.

When we began our excavation there was little ongoing North American tradition in Cretan studies. Unlike the tradition of periodical publication by the French, Italian, and Greek investigators of Cretan culture, North American publication, especially about sites in East Crete (e.g., Gournia, Pseira, Vrokastro,

Kavousi), largely ceased in the 1920s after the group inspired by Harriet Boyd Hawes had passed on. Ours was the first major excavation by North Americans since that early period of activity. But it certainly wasn't about to be the last. Older American excavation sites in East Crete began to be reopened, some as collaborative enterprises with Greek scholars, leading to the establishment of a formal center for study, the INSTAP Study Center for East Crete, founded by Malcolm Wiener.

Some of the earliest explorers in East Crete published their findings under the auspices of their chief official sponsor, the University Museum of the University of Pennsylvania, while some published reports in the *American Journal of Archaeology,* the chief periodical of the Archaeological Institute of America. Beginning in 1932, however, the American School of Classical Studies founded the periodical *Hesperia,* and it became the chief venue for publishing the reports of excavations carried out by the American School, whether independent or in collaboration with Greek colleagues. It was thus understandable that our first report should appear there. There was much to learn, however, before I could write such a report, and it was fortunate that the first summer excavation season in 1976 was followed by a sabbatical year in Athens at the American School. There I had the opportunity to learn from colleagues about certain classes of artifacts, as well as the use of the facilities of the School, especially its splendid scholarly library. The Kommos archives were already substantial, including the record of the field notebooks, the reports written by trench supervisors, by the ceramicists, and even by the cataloguers. This was the first, but by no means the last, sabbatical when excavation records made the trip to Athens on the back seat or in the trunk of a car.

People may assume that it is easy to write a preliminary report. On the contrary, for one must select what is important, follow new topics brought up in the course of digging and research, and simply try to relate specific activities to the past history of work. This must be properly illustrated with photographs and/or drawings such as plans and sections. All must be assembled to send off to the editors. The work, additionally, must be related to what had been done and thought in the past in the area, for instance, by the Italian excavators at Phaistos and Hagia Triada, work begun in the early 1900s, long before people came to excavate at Kommos along the southwestern shore.

At the end of each Kommos report in *Hesperia* there was a section titled "The Historical Context," which introduced some relevant Bronze Age or Classical theme that seemed to merit attention. One function of the preliminary report was that it forced one to try to explain relationships and "phenomena." It could also be used as a "trial balloon," to test explanations. For instance, a flat stone with a depressed circular sinking in it looked to me at one point to be a door pivot, which, in turn, would locate a stairway. This was fully illustrated in a report that was later discarded when it turned out to be impossible. Also, no one knows when an international crisis might make Crete inaccessible for fieldwork and research, or a health problem interfere with or even end work on the site—years of work and money provided generously by organizations and individuals could be lost, perhaps irretrievably. This uncertainty makes published records of progress absolutely mandatory. Within the field itself, previous publication records are basic for any peer-reviewed application for funding.

The foundation for our reports, whether preliminary or final, was the archaeological records. To ensure their quality, trenchmasters were chosen on a competitive basis usually regardless of their university affiliation. The notebooks they wrote were of high quality, bound sheets of graph paper, as functional for drawings as for writing, probably introduced by the American School. They report what really happened in the trenches. If the cost of a season of work were measured by the number of field books used, one for each trench, each book would represent an investment of at least $25,000.

The main records have to be protected, including the notebooks, catalogue cards, databases, etc. These were duplicated, with a complete copy of each kept in both Toronto and Pitsidia. A means of preserving crucial records was adopted in the early 80s, namely putting all notebooks and trench reports on microfiche. We made some eight copies of the entire, labeled series and sent them to the archives of the University of Toronto and the American School, as well as to future contributors to Kommos volumes so that they could conduct their research away from the original records in Toronto or Pitsidia.

Overlapping with conventional typewriters clacking away, the digital revolution arrived. It found me in 1985 being labeled by an unnamed graduate student as a "dinosaur." There wasn't a computer at the excavation, nor had any computer even "looked" at our records. So, chastised, back in Toronto we bought new IBM

PCs, and that was the beginning. We had to learn new "languages"—WordStar, WordPerfect, Word (Maria even learned dBase early on), but our students and children were always ahead of us. Then came e-mail and "attachments," which terrified me when they first began arriving. Yesterday I recollected the miracle when I downloaded in Pitsidia on Crete some three hundred pages of text sent to me from Toronto by our editor Cy Strom, showing the potential path for the future of publishing.

As excavation progressed in the early 80s, and as new houses, some far from each other, were exposed, the Kommos settlement expanded. The Greek Sanctuary was almost completely excavated and we were literally deep into the exploration of the enormous Minoan buildings that perhaps proved to be the greatest surprise of the entire enterprise. It was clear, in any case, that we should be planning for major publication. This was expedited when Joanna Hitchcock of Princeton University Press approached us with the prospect of a series of volumes to be published under their auspices.

It seemed crucial that we should publish the recovered Bronze Age pottery first. Pottery is, after all, the chief indicator of chronology—we always asked our experts the date of the pottery in order to understand new contexts. Other excavators in the Mesara, usually Italian, had proposed a relative chronology using different terminological descriptions. Thus someone describing a house excavated on the Kommos hillside could refer to the ceramic chronology only if they were translated. First Philip Betancourt, then L. Vance Watrous were given priority in our publishing venture, respectively, for significant groups or "deposits" from the site of the Middle and then the Late Bronze Age pottery. Their volumes appeared as *Kommos* II and *Kommos* III, emerging in 1990 and 1992; *Kommos* I (a double volume), a study of the Kommos area, fauna and flora (1) and the town and Minoan domestic economy (2), within what I have called the "Spectrum of Consideration," was not to appear until 1995–1996.

The preparation of such volumes is extremely demanding. The director, an experienced editor, and the contributors must work together sometimes years in advance and then up to the very last moment. The task is complicated by the multidisciplinary approach (discussed in Part II) where geologists, archaeological surveyors, floral and faunal experts, and so many others are involved. Some twenty-seven authors are listed on the title page of Volume I. In retrospect, that list could perhaps have been reduced by a few with the consolidation of assignments, but hard-acquired expertise is needed for an overall evaluation of a site and its contents.

My experience, also, is that while most contributors are "angels," there are some who are definitely from another part of the universe. In these volumes, we are not dealing with a selection of unconnected essays, but rather a series of interconnected studies that are significant only when they are arranged and published together. None can be omitted. Such a collaborative enterprise is difficult and may explain why so many archaeological projects are only represented by monographs on single topics and not on the wider scope of the general excavation itself. Waiting for a final contribution can be excruciating. In one case, an otherwise brilliant contributor had serious emotional ups and downs. After considerable struggle by all concerned, the manuscript eventually arrived and while, in substance, it was excellent many of the hundreds of catalogue numbers were wildly askew. In another instance, the contributor sent us, maddeningly, copies of all his other writings, not the text I requested, and then refused even to reply to my pleas. Then there are always those instances where a manuscript is submitted only after a series of firm deadlines have passed and all the other texts and illustrations are in the hands of the production editor. Perhaps, however, I should focus on the fact that we have had so many angelic colleagues over the years.

The digital world that began for me when I was accused of being a dinosaur has profited us immensely in the ease of transferring and storing data. But then, a reviewer of one of our volumes commented that the book was fine but that it should be in digital form rather than in an expensive hard copy. It was like being called a dinosaur all over again. The question of digital publishing is, however, a real one. Would digital devices and texts be convenient for a researcher sitting at a library table? Or, for those of us who depend on reports printed over a hundred years ago, will such resources exist a hundred years from now if we were to follow that reviewer's advice? That depends upon the information being retained and the methodology for reading it being maintained and updated. There are many "ifs." Even the best compact disks have limited lifetimes.

While we remain committed to hard copy, there is still room for experimentation. As an alternative to eliminating certain data about pottery from our Volume V, we considered providing a compact disk in a sleeve at the back of the book, or including the information on the Kommos website. Our various informal committee members decided on the latter, so we will include that information as a searchable file on the University of Toronto website once it has been properly edited and arranged.

At approximately the same time we were approached about preparing a major digital source for the Kommos Excavations, including all major publications, many minor ones, as well as the excavation records themselves. The project could take years, but we entertained the suggestion seriously. Now, only a year after its inception, numerous articles are already available, as well as most of the Kommos volumes. The website is: https://tspace.library.utoronto.ca/handle/1807/3004. Full access to all relevant documents for research purposes is surely consonant with a project conducted, for the most part, with public funds. The original records, so lovingly and hard won, should of course remain in the custody of the sponsoring university/organization and be available there for consultation.

FURTHER READING

Alexiou, S. 1969. *Minoan Civilization,* Herakleion.

Alexiou, S., and L. von Matt. 1968. *Ancient Crete,* London.

Betancourt, P. P. 1985. *The History of Minoan Pottery,* Princeton.

Branigan, K. 1970. *The Tombs of Mesara,* London.

Burkert, W. 1985. *Greek Religion,* Cambridge, Mass.

Chadwick, J. 1958. *The Decipherment of Linear B,* Cambridge.

———. 1976. *The Mycenaean World,* Cambridge.

Creta antica: Cento anni di archeologia italiana, 1884–1984, Rome 1984.

Cullen, T., ed. 2001. *Aegean Prehistory: A Review* (*American Journal of Archaeology* Suppl. 1), Boston.

Demargne, P. 1964. *The Birth of Greek Art,* New York.

Dickinson, O. T. P. K. 1994. *The Aegean Bronze Age,* Cambridge.

Doumas, C. 1983. *Thera: Pompeii of the Ancient Aegean,* London.

Evans, A. 1921–1936. *The Palace of Minos at Knossos,* 4 vols., London.

Fitton, J. L. 2002. *Minoans,* London.

Graham, J. W. 1987. *The Palaces of Crete,* rev. ed., Princeton.

Hood, S. 1971. *The Minoans: Crete in the Bronze Age,* London.

———. 1978. *The Arts in Prehistoric Greece,* Harmondsworth.

Hutchinson, R. W. 1962. *Prehistoric Crete,* Middlesex.

Immerwahr, S. A. 1990. *Aegean Painting in the Bronze Age,* University Park.

A Land Called Crete: A Symposium in Memory of Harriet Boyd Hawes, 1871–1945, Northampton 1968.

Levi, D. 1976. *Festòs e la civiltà minoica,* 2 vols., Rome.

Lorimer, H. L. 1950. *Homer and the Monuments,* London.

Marinatos, N. 1993. *Minoan Religion: Ritual, Image, and Symbol,* Columbia, S.C.

McDonald, W. A. 1967. *Progress into the Past,* New York.

Pendlebury, J. D. S. 1939. *The Archaeology of Crete: An Introduction,* London.

Pernier, L., and L. Banti. 1947. *Guida degli scavi italiani in Creta,* Rome.

Platon, N. 1971. *Zakros: The Discovery of a Lost Palace of Ancient Crete,* New York.

Prent, M. 2005. *Cretan Sanctuaries and Cults: Continuity and Change from Late Minoan IIIC to the Archaic Period* (Religions in the Graeco-Roman World 154), Leiden.

Preziosi, D., and L. A. Hitchcock. 1999. *Aegean Art and Architecture,* Oxford.

Rackham, O., and J. Moody. 1996. *The Making of the Cretan Landscape,* Manchester.

Renfrew, C. 1972. *The Emergence of Civilisation: The Cyclades and the Aegean in the Third Millennium B.C.,* London.

Rutkowski, B. 1986. *Cult Places of the Aegean,* New Haven.

Sanders, I. F. 1982. *Roman Crete,* London.

Shaw, J. W. 1973. "Minoan Architecture: Materials and Techniques," *Annuario della Scuola Archeologica di Atene* 44, n.s. 33, pp. 1–236.

Smith, W. S. 1965. *Interconnections in the Ancient Near East,* New Haven.

Spanakis, S. 1983. *Crete,* 2 vols., Herakleion.

Warren, P. 1975. *The Aegean Civilizations,* Lausanne.

Willetts, R. F. 1962. *Cretan Cults and Festivals,* London.

BIBLIOGRAPHY

 For the history of the Kommos site, the reader is first referred to *The Palace of Minos at Knossos* by Sir Arthur Evans (vol. 2, pp. 88–92), who first pointed out the site in 1924. Detailed reporting of the excavation that the University of Toronto began fifty-two years later can be found in a series of monographs, some edited by J. W. and M. C. Shaw and listed below, published by Princeton University Press. The first (I.1, 1995) places the Kommos site within a topographical and geological spectrum, examines the area's ancient and modern fauna and flora, and Minoan industries. The second (I.2, 1996) introduces the houses excavated and their domestic economies. Volumes II (1990) and III (1992) are studies by P. P. Betancourt and L. V. Watrous, respectively, of the Middle and Late Minoan pottery. Volume IV (2000) is a broad study of the architecture and stratigraphy, inscriptions, pottery, sculpture, flora, fauna, and miscellaneous finds from the Greek Sanctuary. Volume V, a summary volume and the final one in the Princeton series, reports on and interprets the architecture and stratigraphy, plasters, pottery, and other finds from the monumental Minoan buildings in the Southern Area. Additionally, the Minoan pottery kiln in the South Stoa is studied in J. W. Shaw et al. 2001. A separate monograph is being prepared by M. C. Shaw, J. B. Rutter, and J. W. Shaw for House X north of the east-west paved Minoan road. Various studies by staff members are included in the list below. Some of these publications can be found only in university libraries, but can be obtained through interlibrary loan.

Monographs in the Kommos Series

Kommos = Kommos: An Excavation on the South Coast of Crete by the University of Toronto and the Royal Ontario Museum under the Auspices of the American School of Classical Studies at Athens, Princeton

  I.1 = J. W. Shaw and M. C. Shaw, eds., *The Kommos Region and Houses of the Minoan Town: The Kommos Region, Ecology, and Minoan Industries,* 1995.

  I.2 = J. W. Shaw and M. C. Shaw, eds., *The Kommos Region and Houses of the Minoan Town: The Minoan Hilltop and Hillside Houses,* 1996.

  II = P. P. Betancourt, *The Final Neolithic through the Middle Minoan III Pottery,* 1990.

  III = L. V. Watrous, *The Late Bronze Age Pottery,* 1992.

  IV = J. W. Shaw and M. C. Shaw, eds., *The Greek Sanctuary,* 2000.

  V = J. W. Shaw and M. C. Shaw, eds., *The Monumental Minoan Buildings,* in press.

Chapters in Monographs and Separate Articles

Anderson, P. 2000. "A Human Skull from Kommos, Crete," in *Kommos* IV, pp. 407–414.

Bennet, J. 1994. "Two New Marks on Bronze Age Pottery from Kommos," *Kadmos* 33, pp. 153–159.

———. 1996. "Catalogue of Miscellaneous Finds: Marks on Bronze Age Pottery from Kommos," in *Kommos* I.2, pp. 313–321.

Betancourt, P. P. 1980. *Cooking Vessels from Minoan Kommos: A Preliminary Report* (Institute of Archaeology, University of California, Los Angeles, Occasional Paper 7), Los Angeles.

———. 1985. "A Great Minoan Triangle: The Changing Characters of Phaistos, Hagia Triadha, and Kommos during the Middle Minoan–Late Minoan III Periods," in Shaw and Shaw 1985, pp. 31–34.

Betancourt, P. P., L. Berkowitz, and R. L. Zaslow. 1990. "Evidence for a Minoan Basket from Kommos, Crete," *Cretan Studies* 2, pp. 73–77.

Bianco, G. 2003. "Two Different Building Modules of Measurement at Kommos: Neopalatial Module in Building T and a Postpalatial Module in Building P," in *Metron: Measuring the Aegean Bronze Age* (Aegaeum 24), ed. K. Foster and R. Laffineur, Liège, pp. 415–419.

Bikai, P. M. 2000. "The Phoenician Ceramics from the Greek Sanctuary," in *Kommos* IV, pp. 302–321.

Blitzer, H. B. 1995. "Minoan Implements and Industries," in *Kommos* I.1, pp. 403–535.

Buxeda i Garrigos, J., V. Kilikoglou, and P. M. Day. 2001. "Chemical and Mineralogical Alteration of Ceramics from a Late Bronze Age Kiln at Kommos, Crete: The Effect on the Formation of a Control Group," *Archaeometry* 43, pp. 349–371.

Callaghan, P. J., A. Johnston, J. W. Hayes, and R. Jones. 2000. "The Iron Age Pottery from Kommos," in *Kommos* IV, pp. 210–335.

Csapo, E. 1991. "An International Community of Traders in Late 8th–7th c. B.C. Kommos in Southern Crete," *Zeitschrift für Papyrologie und Epigraphik* 88, pp. 211–216.

———. 1993. "A Postscript to 'An International Community of Traders in Late 8th–7th c. B.C. Kommos in Southern Crete,'" *Zeitschrift für Papyrologie und Epigraphik* 96, pp. 235–236.

Csapo, E., A. W. Johnston, and D. Geagan. 2000. "The Iron Age Inscriptions," in *Kommos* IV, pp. 101–134.

Dabney, M. K. 1996. "Catalogue of Miscellaneous Finds: Ceramic Loomweights and Spindle Whorls," "Jewellery and Seals," and "Lead Objects," in *Kommos* I.2, pp. 244–270.

———. 2000. "Jewellery," and "Ceramic Loomweights and Spindle Whorls," in *Kommos* IV, pp. 341–350, 352–357.

Day, P. M., and V. Kilikoglou. 2001. "Analysis of Ceramics from the Kiln," in Shaw et al. 2001, pp. 111–134.

Gifford, J. 1995. "The Physical Geology of the Western Mesara and Kommos," in *Kommos* I.1, pp. 30–90.

Hayes, J. W. 2000. "Roman Pottery from the Sanctuary," "Roman Lamps from the Sanctuary," and "Glass," in *Kommos* IV, pp. 312–320, 320–330, 336–340.

Hope Simpson, R., et al. 1995. "The Archaeological Survey of the Kommos Area," in *Kommos* I.1, pp. 325–402.

Johnston, A. W. 1992. "Anfore laconiche a Kommos," in *Lakonikà: Ricerche e nuovi materiali di ceramica laconica,* ed. P. Pelagatti (*Bollettino d'arte* Suppl. 64), Rome, pp. 115–116.

———. 1993. "Pottery from Archaic Building Q at Kommos," *Hesperia* 62, pp. 339–382.

———. 2000. "Building Z at Kommos: An 8th-Century Pottery Sequence," *Hesperia* 69, pp. 189–226.

Johnston, A. W., and T. de Domingo. 1997. "Trade between Kommos, Crete, and East Greece: A Petrographic Study of Archaic Transport Amphorae," in *Archaeological Sciences 1995. Proceedings of a Conference on the Application of Scientific Techniques to the Study of Archaeology, Liverpool, July 1995,* ed. A. Sinclair, E. Slater, and J. Gowlett, Oxford, pp. 62–68.

Joyner, L., and P. M. Day. 2001. "The Kommos LM IA Kiln: Petrographic Fabric Descriptions," in Shaw et al. 2001, pp. 139–155.

La Rosa, V. 1985. "Preliminary Considerations on the Problem of the Relationship between Phaistos and Hagia Triadha," in Shaw and Shaw 1985, pp. 45–54.

McEnroe, J. 1996. "The Central Hillside at Kommos: The Late Minoan Period," in *Kommos* I.2, pp. 199–235.

Nixon, L. F. 1996. "The Oblique House and the Southeast Rooms," in *Kommos* I.2, pp. 59–92.

Parsons, M. 1995. "Soil and Land Use Studies at Kommos," in *Kommos* I.1, pp. 292–324.

Payne, S. 1995. "The Small Mammals," in *Kommos* I.1, pp. 278–291.

Puglisi, D. 2001. "Un arsenale marittimo l'edificio T di Kommòs?" *Creta antica* 2, pp. 113–124.

Raumer, J. W. F., and S. Payne. 1986. "Notes on the *Soricidae* (Insectovora, Mammalia) from Crete, II: The Shrew Remains from Minoan and Classical Kommos," *Bonner zoologische Beiträge* 37, pp. 173–182.

Reese, D. 1995. "The Minoan Fauna," in *Kommos* I.1, pp. 163–291.

———. 2000. "Worked Astragali," "Ostrich Eggshell," and "Fossils," in *Kommos* IV, pp. 398–401, 401–403, 403–407.

Reese, D., M. J. Rose, and D. Ruscillo. 2000. "The Iron Age Fauna," in *Kommos* IV, pp. 415–646.

Rehder, J. E. 2000. "Ironworking in the Greek Sanctuary," in *Kommos* IV, pp. 80–89.

Rose, M. J. 1995. "The Fish Remains," in *Kommos* I.1, pp. 204–240.

———. 2000. "The Fish Remains," in *Kommos* IV, pp. 495–560.

Ruscillo, D. In press. "Faunal Remains and *Murex* Dye Production," in *Kommos* V.

Russell, P. J. 1985. "A Middle Cypriote Jug from Kommos, Crete," in *Temple University Aegean Symposium* 10, ed. P. P. Betancourt, Philadelphia, pp. 42–50.

Rutter, J. 1999. "Cretan External Relations during LM IIIA2–B (ca. 1370–1200 B.C.): A View from the Mesara," in *The Point Iria Wreck: Interconnections in the Mediterranean, ca. 1200 B.C.*, ed. W. Phelps, Y. Lolos, and Y. Vichos, Athens, pp. 139–186.

———. 2000. "The Short-Necked Amphora of the Post-Palatial Mesara," Πεπραγμένα του Θ' Διεθνούς Κρητολογικού Συνεδρίου, Ηράκλειο, 9–14 Σεπτεμβρίου, 1996, Herakleion, pp. 177–188.

———. 2004. "Ceramic Sets in Context: One Dimension of Food Preparation and Consumption in a Minoan Palatial Setting," in *Food, Cuisine, and Society in Prehistoric Greece* (Sheffield Studies in Archaeology 5), ed. P. Halstead and J. C. Barrett, Oxford, pp. 63–89.

———. 2004. "Off-island Imports to Kommos, Crete: New Discoveries and Identifications; Old Problems Unresolved," *Bulletin of the Institute of Classical Studies of the University of London* 47, pp. 189–190.

———. In press. "Ceramic Imports of the Neopalatial Bronze Age Eras and Later," in *Kommos* V.

———. In press. "Minoan Pottery from the Southern Area," in *Kommos* V.

Schwab, K. A. 1996. "Catalogue of Miscellaneous Finds: Stone Vessels," in *Kommos* I.2, pp. 271–282.

———. 2000. "Bronze, Lead, and Bone Implements," and "Bronze, Lead, and Faience Vessels," in *Kommos* IV, pp. 391–395, 395–398.

Sease, C. 1996. "Objects Conservation at Kommos," in *Kommos* I.2, pp. 326–328.

Shaw, J. W. 1981. "Kommos: The Southern Port of Entry into Central Crete," *ROM Archaeological Newsletter*, n.s. 196, n.p.

———. 1983. "The Development of Minoan Orthostates," *American Journal of Archaeology* 87, pp. 213–216.

———. 1983. "Stone Weight Anchors from Kommos, Crete," *International Journal of Nautical Archaeology and Underwater Exploration*, pp. 91–100.

———. 1984. "Minoan Kommos: A Harbour Town of Ancient Crete," *Rotunda* 7, pp. 24–33.

———. 1984. "A New Colonnade Discovered at Kommos, Crete," *ROM Archaeological Newsletter* II(2), n.p.

———. 1986. "Excavations at Kommos (Crete) during 1984–1985," *Hesperia* 55, pp. 219–269.

———. 1987. "A 'Palatial' Stoa at Kommos," in *The Function of the Minoan Palaces. Proceedings of the Fourth International Symposium at the Swedish Institute in Athens, 10–16 June 1984,* ed. R. Hägg and N. Marinatos, Stockholm, pp. 101–109.

———. 1989. "Phoenicians in Southern Crete," *American Journal of Archaeology* 93, pp. 165–183.

———. 1990. "Bronze Age Aegean Harborsides," in *Thera and the Aegean World* III. *Proceedings of the Third International Congress, Santorini, Greece, 3–9 September 1989,* ed. D. A. Hardy, London, vol. 1, pp. 420–436.

———. 1991. "North American Archaeological Work in Crete (1880–1990)," *Expedition* 32, pp. 5–14.

———. 1995. "The Exploration and Excavation of the Kommos Site," in *Kommos* I.1, pp. 8–29.

———. 1995. "Two Three-holed Stone Anchors from Kommos, Crete: Their Context, Type, and Origin," *International Journal of Nautical Archaeology and Underwater Exploration* 24, pp. 279–291.

———. 1996. "Introduction to the Kommos Site," and "Domestic Economy and Site Development," in *Kommos* I.2, pp. 1–14, 379–400.

———. 1998. "Kommos in Southern Crete: An Aegean Barometer for East–West Interconnections," in *Eastern Mediterranean: Cyprus-Dodecanese-Crete, 16th–6th Cent. B.C.,* ed. V. Karageorghis and N. Stampolidis, Athens, pp. 13–27.

———. 1998. "Der phönizische Schrein in Kommos auf Kreta (ca. 800 v. Chr.)," *Veröffentlichung der Joachim Jungius-Gesellschaft der Wissenschaften Hamburg* 87, pp. 93–104.

———. 1999. "A Tale of Three Bases: New Criteria for Dating Minoan Architectural Features," in *Meletemata: Studies in Aegean Archaeology Presented to Malcolm H. Wiener As He Enters His 65th Year* (*Aegaeum* 20), ed. P. P. Betancourt, V. Karageorghis, R. Laffineur, and W.-D. Niemeier, Liège, pp. 761–767.

———. 2000. "The Architecture of the Temples and Other Buildings," "Sanctuary Furnishings," "Bronze and Iron Nails," "Stone Implements," and "Ritual and Development in the Greek Sanctuary," in *Kommos* IV, pp. 1–100, 358–363, 373–386, 386–391, 669–731.

———. 2000. "The Phoenician Shrine, ca. 800 B.C., at Kommos in Crete," *Actas del IV Congreso Internacional de Estudios Fenicios y Púnicos,* Cadiz, pp. 1107–1119.

———. 2000. "Pilgrims at the Greek Sanctuary at Kommos," in Πεπραγμένα του Θ' Διεθνούς Κρητολογικού Συνεδρίου, Ἡράκλειο, *9–14 Σεπτεμβρίου, 1996,* Herakleion, pp. 219–226.

———. 2001. "The Excavation and the Structure of the Kiln," in Shaw et al. 2001, pp. 5–24.

———. 2001. "The Mystery of the Pitsidian Slab," in *Ithaki: Festschrift für Jörg Schäfer zum 75. Geburtstag am 25. April 2001,* ed. S. Bohm and K.-V. von Eickstedt, pp. 137–142.

———. 2002. "The Minoan Palatial Establishment at Kommos: An Anatomy of Its History, Function, and Interconnections," in *Monuments of Minos: Rethinking the Minoan Palaces* (*Aegaeum* 23), ed. J. Driessen, I. Schoep, and R. Laffineur, Liège, pp. 99–110.

———. 2003. "Palatial Proportions: A Study of the Relative Proportions between Minoan Palaces and their Settlements," in *Metron: Measuring the Aegean Bronze Age* (*Aegaeum* 24), ed. K. Foster and R. Laffineur, Liège, pp. 239–245.

———. 2004. "Kommos: The Sea-Gate to Southern Crete," in *Crete Beyond the Palaces. Proceedings of the Crete 2000 Conference,* ed. L. P. Day, M. S. Mook, and J. D. Muhly, Philadelphia, pp. 43–52.

———. In press. "The Architecture and Stratigraphy of the Civic Buildings," and "The History and Functions of the Monumental Minoan Buildings at Kommos," in *Kommos* V.

———. In press. "Metals and Metalworking," "Loomweights and Miscellaneous Clay Objects," "Items of Adornment," "Artifacts of Stone," in *Kommos* V.

Shaw, J. W., and D. Harlan. 2000. "Bronze and Iron Tools and Weapons," in *Kommos* IV, pp. 363–373.

Shaw, J. W., and M. C. Shaw. 1981. "Excavations at Kommos and Recent Discoveries in Crete," *Rotunda* 14, pp. 12–19.

———. 1993. "Excavations at Kommos (Crete) during 1986–1992," *Hesperia* 62, pp. 129–190.

———. 1997. "Mycenaean Kommos," in *La Crète mycénienne* (*Bulletin de correspondance hellénique* Suppl. 30), ed. J. Driessen and A. Farnoux, Athens, pp. 423–434.

———. 1999. "A Proposal for Bronze Age Aegean Ship-sheds in Crete," in *Tropis V. 5th International Symposium on Ship Construction in Antiquity,* ed. H. Tzalas, Athens, pp. 369–382.

———. 2000. "Minoan and Greek Kommos: An Excavation on the South Coast of Crete by Canadian and American Archaeologists," in *One Hundred Years of American Archaeological Work on Crete,* ed. J. Muhly and E. Sikla, Athens, pp. 160–178.

Shaw, J. W., and M. C. Shaw, eds. 1985. *A Great Minoan Triangle in South-Central Crete: Kommos, Hagia Triadha, Phaistos* (Scripta Mediterranea VI), Toronto.

Shaw, J. W., and M. Shaw-Coutroubaki. 2000. "Κομμός: Η Θέση του στην προιστορική και την ιστορική εποχή," in *Η Μεσαρά μέσα απο τα μνημεία της. Πρώτη Αρχαιολογική Συνάντηση Μεσαράς, Μοίρες, 5–7 Σεπτεμβρίου 1996,* ed. A. Vasilakis, Moires, pp. 64–110.

Shaw, J. W., A. Van de Moortel, P. M. Day, and V. Kilikoglou. 1997. "A LM IA Kiln at Kommos, Crete," in *Techne: Craftsmen, Craftswomen, and Craftsmanship in the Aegean Bronze Age* (*Aegaeum* 16), ed. R. Laffineur and P. P. Betancourt, Liège, pp. 323–330.

———. 2001. *A LM IA Ceramic Kiln in South-Central Crete: Function and Pottery Production* (*Hesperia* Suppl. 30), Princeton.

Shaw, M. C. 1981. "Sir Arthur Evans at Kommos: A Cretan Village Remembers Its Past," *Expedition* 23, pp. 4–12.

———. 1983. "Two Cups with Incised Decoration from Kommos, Crete," *American Journal of Archaeology* 87, pp. 443–452.

———. 1985. "Late Minoan I Building J/T, and Late Minoan III Buildings N and P at Kommos: Their Nature and Possible Uses as Residences, Palaces, and/or Emporia," in Shaw and Shaw 1985, pp. 19–30.

———. 1987. "A Bronze Figurine of a Man from the Sanctuary at Kommos, Crete," in Ειλαπίνη: *Τόμος τιμητικός για τον καθηγητή Νικόλαο Πλάτωνα,* ed. L. Kastrinaki, G. Orphanou, and N. Giannadakis, Herakleion, pp. 371–382.

———. 1990. "Late Minoan Hearths and Ovens at Kommos, Crete," in *L'habitat égéen préhistorique* (*Bulletin de correspondance hellénique* Suppl. 19), ed. P. Darcque and R. Treuil, Athens, pp. 231–254.

———. 1991. "Back to Kommos and the 1991 Campaign: A View from House X," *ROM Archaeological Newsletter* II(46), n.p.

———. 1996. "Introduction," "The North House and Peripheral Areas," "The Southern Cliffside," "The House with the Press," in *Kommos* I.2, pp. 15–59, 92–105, 105–138.

———. 1996. "Terracotta Sculpture," in *Kommos* I.2, pp. 282–302.

———. 1996. "Town Plasters," in *Kommos* I.2, pp. 303–313.

———. 1999. "A Bronze Age Enigma: The 'U-Shaped' Motif in Aegean Architectural Representations," in *Meletemata: Studies in Aegean Archaeology Presented to Malcolm H. Wiener As He Enters His 65th Year* (*Aegaeum* 20), ed. P. P. Betancourt, V. Karageorghis, R. Laffineur, and W.-D. Niemeier, Liège, pp. 769–779.

———. 2000. "The Sculpture from the Sanctuary," in *Kommos* IV, pp. 135–209.

———. 2004. "Religion at Minoan Kommos," in *Crete Beyond the Palaces. Proceedings of the Crete 2000 Conference,* ed. L. P. Day, M. S. Mook, J. D. Muhly, Philadelphia, pp. 137–152.

———. In press. "Plasters from the Monumental Minoan Buildings as Evidence for Painted Decoration, Architectural Appearance, and Archaeological Event," in *Kommos* V.

———. In press. "Plaster Offering Tables," in *Kommos* V.

———. In press. "Figurines and Figural Clay Attachments," in *Kommos* V.

Shaw, M. C., J. B. Rutter, and J. W. Shaw, eds. In prep. *Kommos: House X.*

Shay, C. T., and J. M. Shay, with K. A. Frego and J. Zwiazek. 1995. "The Modern Flora and Plant Remains from Bronze Age Deposits at Kommos," in *Kommos* I.1, pp. 91–162.

———. 2000. "The Charcoal and Seeds from Iron Age Kommos," in *Kommos* IV, pp. 647–668.

Skon-Jedele, N., and M. Dabney. 2000. "Scarabs," in *Kommos* IV, p. 351.

Van de Moortel, A. 1997. "The Transition from the Protopalatial to the Neopalatial Society in South-Central Crete: A Ceramic Perspective" (diss. Bryn Mawr College).

———. 2001. "The Area around the Kiln, and the Pottery from the Kiln and the Kiln Dump," in Shaw et al. 2001, pp. 25–110.

———. In press. "Ceramic Imports of the Protopalatial Era," in *Kommos* V.

———. In press. "Minoan Pottery from the Southern Area," in *Kommos* V.

Walker, A. 2000. "Coins," in *Kommos* IV, pp. 340–341.

Watrous, L. V. 1985. "Late Bronze Age Kommos: Imported Pottery as Evidence for Foreign Contact," in Shaw and Shaw 1985, pp. 7–11.

———. 1989. "A Preliminary Report on Imported 'Italian' Wares from the Late Bronze Age Site of Kommos on Crete," *Studi micenei ed egeo-anatolici* 27, pp. 69–79.

Watrous, L. V., et al. 1993. "A Survey of the Western Mesara Plain in Crete: Preliminary Report of the 1984, 1986, and 1987 Field Seasons," *Hesperia* 62, pp. 191–248.

Watrous, L. V., P. M. Day, and R. Jones. 1998. "The Sardinian Pottery from the Late Bronze Age Site of Kommos in Crete: Description, Chemical and Petrographic Analyses, and Historical Context," in *Sardinian and Aegean Chronology: Towards the Resolution of Relative and Absolute Dating in the Mediterranean* (Studies in Sardinian Archaeology 5), ed. M. S. Balmuth and R. H. Tykot, Oxford, pp. 337–340.

Watrous, L. V., D. Hadzi-Vallianou, and H. Blitzer. 2004. *The Plain of Phaistos: Cycles of Social Complexity in the Mesara Region of Crete* (Monumenta Archaeologica 23), Los Angeles.

Whittaker, H. 1996. "Catalogue of Miscellaneous Finds: Stone Slabs with Depressions," and "Block Vases," in *Kommos* I.2, pp. 321–323, 323–324.

Wright, J. C. 1996. "The Central Hillside at Kommos, The Middle Minoan Period," in *Kommos* I.2, pp. 140–199.

CREDITS

The following publishers have generously given permission to use extended quotations from copyrighted works.

P. 59. Ll. 292–300 from Book 3 of *The Odyssey*, translated by R. Lattimore, courtesy HarperCollins Publishers, Copyright 1965 by Harper and Row.

P. 131. Reprinted by permission of the publishers of the Loeb Classical Library from Athenaeus of Naucratis: *The Deipnosophists*, 9:371–375 (on hogs), translated by C. B. Gulick, Cambridge: Harvard University Press, 1928.

Illustrations

All site photographs are by J. W. Shaw unless noted otherwise.

Figs. 3a&b, 4, 5, 6, 9, 14, 15, 20, 21, 22, 26, 27, 29, 33, 37, 38, 41, 45, 57, 58, 59, 60, 72 by G. Bianco; Fig. 46 by T. Boyd; Cover and Figs. 2, 36, 39, 40, 42, 44, 51, 52, 53, 55, 56 by T. Dabney; Fig. 76 by D. Gardner; Fig. 61 by J. W. Graham; Endpaper plan by M. Nelson and G. Bianco; Fig. 7 by J. Phillips; Fig. 1 by A. C. Shaw; Fig. 31 by J. W. Shaw and G. Bianco; Fig. 16 by M. C. Shaw; Fig. 10 by M. C. Shaw and G. Bianco; Fig. 54 by D. H. Simpson; Fig. 35 by R. K. Vincent Jr.

INDEX

Page numbers appearing in *italic* type refer to pages that contain illustrations.

"A Great Minoan Triangle" (conference), 79–81, 124
Alexiou, Stylianos (Ephor of Herakleion Museum and 23rd Ephorate in central Crete), 105, 106
alphabet, Greek adaptation of, 140
Altar C, 12, 47, *48*, 88. *See also* Temple C
Altar H, 45, 47. *See also* Temple C
Altar L, 49
Altar M, 49
American Journal of Archaeology, 111, 127, 145
American School of Classical Studies at Athens (ASCSA), 9, 88, 100, 145
    excavation permit, 106, 107
Amnisos, 54, 55, 105
amphoras, 24, 57
    in Building Q, 43
    short-necked, *39*
Amrhein, Carl (Dean of Arts and Sciences, University of Toronto), 98
Anapodaria (ancient Potherious) River, 72
anchor dance, 94
anchors, 56–57
    discovery in Building P, 94
    faces and section of, *95*
    marble stock of, 578
    petrological composition of, 94–95
anti-tank mines, 86
anvils, stone, 129
Apollo, 50, 140
Apollo, Temple of (Dreros), 136, *137*, 138
Archaeological Institute of America, 79, 145
    Toronto Branch, 97

archaeological landscapes, 62
architecture
    characteristics of Minoan palaces, 119
    "Dreros" type temples, 136, *137*, 138, 141
    orientation of temples, 41
    palaces as civic centers, 73, 74
Artemis (Diana), 50, 140
    prayer to, 135
    temple dedicated to, 134–35
artifact "families," 116–17, 138, 141
ashlar blocks
    reuse of, 38
    robbing of, 132
Asklepios, Temple of (Lissos), 136, *137*, 138
Athena, inscription to, 49–50, 133
Athenaeus of Naucratis, on eating pigs, 131
Athens
    harbors of, 53, 103
    pottery from, 43, 57, 139

Babiniotakis, George, 122
Bandekas, John, 105
basins, stone (perirrhanteria), 45, 49, 132
Bass, George F., 103
Beladakis, George, 69, 86, 108, *109*, 134–35
Betancourt, John, 67
Betancourt, Mary, 67
Betancourt, Michael, 67
Betancourt, Philip, 80, 92, 111, 147
Bianco, Giuliana, 9, 67, 89, *90*
    sketches of Pitsidia, *66*, *67*, *69*, *70*
Bikai, Patricia, 116
Bikakis, Harry, 69, 88

bins, stone, 34
Blackman, D., 124
Blitzer, Harriet, *64,* 129
bowl, incised black glazed, 43, 140
bowl, Minoan offering, 49
Boyd (later Hawes), Harriet, 96, 105, 145
Broneer, Oscar, 101, 102
bronze
    bull figurine, 43, *44*
    cult figurines from Dreros, 140
    dress/hair pins, 49
    fishhooks, 56, 130
    horse bit, 140
    horse figurine, 43, *44,* 89, *90,* 139, 140
    ingots, 117
    laurel wreath with ivory berries, 49, *50*
    metalworking, 34
    net mender, 56
    scrap from Sardinia, 116
    shield, *42,* 43, 140
    tools, 24, 29, 93
Building AA, 11, 79
    function of, 118
    platform of, 30
    ritual use of, 30
Building J. *See* Building T
Building N, 37
    function of, 75
    imported wares and, 118
    sea levels and, 56
Building P, 11, 138
    anchors from, 94
    construction of, 38, 75
    discovery of, 13
    galleries of, 38, 39
    imported wares and function of, 118
    orthostate façades of T in, 38
    plan of, *37*
    restored view of, *38*
    reused anchors from, 57
    sea levels and, 56
    as shipsheds, 39, 79–80, 124–25, 141, 142
    and short-necked amphoras, 39
    storage function of, 124, 125
Building Q, 11, 43, *45,* 57
Building T, 11, 30–35, 141. *See also* Central Court; North Stoa; South Stoa
    components of, 120
    construction of, 74, 79
    discovery of, 12–13, 90–92

    eastern façade of, 123
    eastern wing of, 34–35
    erosion by waves, 55–56
    excavation in 1993, *93*
    fire damage in, 34–35
    function of, 35
    northwestern entrance, *91*
    NW entrance to, 33
    orthostate façades, 30, *31,* 33
    as palace, 119
    plan of, *32,* 34
    restored view of NW entrance to, *33*
    reuse of elements in Building P, 38
    reuse of elements in Temple A, 41
    Room 5, 92
    southern wall of, 122
    storerooms in, 34, 35
bull figurine, bronze, 43, *44*
bull figurine, terracotta, 47, *48,* 87–88
Buondelmonti, Cristoforo, 135

Canada Council, 97
Cape Gelidonya shipwreck, 59
Cape Lithinos, 51, 59
Carthage (Tunisia), 53, 103
catfish, freshwater *(Clarias gariepinos),* 130
cattle remains, 128, 131
Central Court, 33
    discovery of, 13, 120–22
    excavation of southern border, 70, 122
    stratigraphy of, 30
ceramic chronology
    House X stratified sequences and, 29
Chania, 61, 107
    LM II pottery from, 127
cobbles (hammer stones), 18, 128
column bases
    Minoan, 33, 35, *36,* 120, 121, 122
    in Temple C, 41, 45, 89
containers, oil or perfume (unguentaria), 49
cooking and food preparation, 18, 47, 128–31
copper ingots, 117
Corinth, 101
    pottery from, 43, 57, 139
Coutroubaki, Maria. *See* Shaw, Maria C.
Cox, William, *48*
Crete
    in Greek period, 77
    map of major Greek and Roman sites, *17*
    map of major Minoan sites, *17*

as Roman province, 77–78
Csapo, Eric, 39
cult statues and bases, 47, 49, 132
　bronze laurel wreath with ivory berries, 49, *50*
　ivory eye, 49, 132
Cyclops, 57
Cyprus
　anchors from, 95
　imported wares from, 18, 75, 93, 94, 115
　pithoi in House X, *58*
Cyrenaica, 77

Dabney, Taylor, 9
Daskalakis, Manolis, 88, 105
Day, Leslie, 107
Deipnosophists, The (Athenaeus of Naucratis), 131
deities, trinities of, 50
de Jong, Piet, 101
dietary evidence, 128
domestic economy, 96, 128–31, 141
　recent ethnographic parallels, 128–30
Dreros
　bronze cult figurines from, 140
　Geometric Temple of Apollo, 47, 136, *137*, 138
dress/hair pins, bronze, 49

earthquakes, 18, 35
Eastman Kodak Company, 97
Egyptian imports
　Nefertum figurine, 43, 139
　pottery, 57, 116, 117
　salted fish, 130
　Sekhmet figurine, 43, *44*, 139, 140
Eleutherna, Phoenician finds from, 140
Evangelistria, church of, 134
　views of, *113*, *134*
Evans, Dame Joan, 103, 144
Evans, John, 97
Evans, Sir Arthur
　on the "customs house" *(teloneion)* in Kommos, 103
　focus of work, 96, 144
　on Kommos, 12, 103, 104
　Minoan periodization by, 11, 80
　and "Palace Style" wares, 126
excavations at Kommos
　archaeological survey walks by J. W. Shaw, 104, 134–35
　discovery of Greco-Roman wall, 87
　excavation staff, 66, 67

financing, 97–99
large Minoan buildings in 1993, *93*
Pitsidia villagers as excavation staff, 67
pre-dawn approach to site, 84–85
provisions and equipment for, 108
records and archives, 101, 145, 146–47
research aims, 92, 96, 115, 116
sand clearing, 12, 85–87, 122, 141–42
selection criteria for trenchmasters, 66, 146
techniques, 23
excavations in rural and urban areas, 62

faience figurines, 43, *44*, 89, 139, 140
Fasoulakis, Aristotle, *109*
Fasoulakis, Iannis, 89, *109*
Fasoulakis, Sifis, *109*, 120–21
faunal remains, 128, 130–31
Fieldiana, 100
field surveys, 62
fire damage, 34–35
fishhooks, bronze, 56, 130
fishing
　evidence for, 56, 130
　explosives and, 86
fish remains, 56
flora of Kommos, 128
frescoes
　colored stripes (T19), 34
　lilies (House X), *28, 29,* 74, 93–94
Frost, Robert, 143

Galatas
　palace of, 119
Gavdos pottery, 117
Gebhard, Betsy, 101
George (night guard at Kommos), 87
Geropotamos (ancient Lethaios) River, 72
Gesell, Geraldine, 107, 111
Gifford, John, 55
goat/sheep remains, 128, 131
Gortyn, 47, 50, 62
　as capital of Roman province, 77–78
　Temple of Apollo, *77*, 91
Gournia, 96
grain
　grinding methods, 34, 128
　Postpalatial collection of, 76
Greek Antiquities Service, 9, 101, 135
　and development restrictions around Kommos, 68

Greek Oared Ships 900-322 B.C. (Blackman), 124
Greek Sanctuary, 41–50, 141. *See also* Temple A;
    Temple B; Temple C; Tripillar Shrine
    Altar C, 12, 47, *48*, 88
    Altar H, 45, 47
    Altar L, 49
    Altar M, 49
    Banquet Room A1, *46*, 47, 49
    Building B, 47, *48*
    deities worshipped, 49–50, 132–33, 139, 140
    discovery of, 87–88, 111
    discovery of Altar C, 12, 88
    hearths used as altars, 41
    hiatus in activities, 45
    model of, *40*
    and nearby settlement, 43
    orientation of temples within, 41
    ritual meals and sacrifices, 45, 57, 128
    round enclosure (D), 47
    stratigraphy of, 30, 41
    view from southeast, *40*
    warden ("neokoros") of, 47
grinding of grain, 34, 128

Hagia Galene (ancient Soulia), 51, 134
Hagia Irini (Kea), 53
Hagia Triada, 145
    as administrative center, 76
    commercial activities at, 76
    as "da-wo," 76
    destruction of, 74
    Greek remains at, 78
    megaron (ABCD), 76
    in Neopalatial Period, 79
    new construction in LM IIIA2, 76
    prehistoric settlement of, 73, 74, *75*
    shrine, 76
    stoa (EF), 76
Hagia Varvara, 108
Hagios Pandeleimon (St. Pandeleimon), church
    of, 84, 143
Ham, James (President, University of Toronto),
    98
harbors
    Bronze Age types, 53, 55
    history in the Mediterranean, 103
hearths, 23, 24, 29
    in Banquet Room A1, 47
    in Building B of Greek Sanctuary, 47
    slab stands and, 131

    in Temple C, *42*, 45, 136
    used as altars, 41
Herakleion, 63, 72, 95
Herakleion Archaeological Museum, 102
Hesperia, 120, 122, 145, 146
Higgins Flat Pueblo, 100
hillside houses, 18, 23
    excavation of, 27, 29
    plan of, *21*
    renewal of, 35
    Room 25, 18
hilltop houses, 18
    courts within, 24
    excavation of, 23–24
    LM I court, 18, 23
    plan of, *20*
    Sardinian collar-necked jar from, *58*
History of Art Department, University of
    Toronto, 97
History of Seafaring, A (Bass, ed.), 103
Hitchcock, Joanna, 147
Homer
    on shipsheds, 39
    on the shipwreck of Menelaos, 59
Hope Simpson, Richard (Dick), 104
horse bit, bronze, 140
horse figurine, bronze, 43, *44*, 89, *90*, 139, 140
horses, terracotta, 140
House with the Snake Tube
    LM II pottery from, 126, *127*
    restored view of Room 4, *27*
    stamnostatis (stone slab base), 129, *130*
    stratified dumps of, 126
House X
    construction of, 74
    Cypriot pithoi, *58*
    discovery of, 13, 92–93
    evidence for fishing in, 56
    excavation of, 29, *83*
    function of, 29
    lily fresco, *28*, 29, 74, 93–94
    short-necked amphora from, *39*

Illinois Institute of Technology, 101
imported wares
    ceramic sequences and monumental
        buildings, 118
    from Cyprus, 18, 57, *58*, 75, 93, 94, 115, 116
    decanting contents of large storage vessels, 117
    domestic use in Kommos, 117, 141

from Egypt, 57
identification and analysis of, 115–18
Knossian vessels, 115
and overseas trade, 57, 80, 94, 118
Phoenician vessels, 43, 90, 116, 140
from Sardinia, 37, 57, 75, 80, 94, 116
from Syria, 57, 75, 94
and "The Strange and Wonderful" box, 115, 116
unknown provenance of, 116
Western Anatolian vessels, 117. 43
inscription on slab, Temple C, 49–50, 133
INSTAP Study Center for East Crete, 145
Institute for Aegean Prehistory, 9, 97
International Harvester van (The Armadillo), 84, 108
Isthmia, sanctuary of Poseidon, 101, 102
ivory berries and bronze laurel wreath, 49, *50*
ivory eye, 49

Jarkiewicz, Zbigniew, 99

Kadianaki, Theonifi, 128
Kadianakis, Manolis, *109*, 110
Kalamaki, 71, 104, 134, 135
Kaloi Limenes, 53, 72
Kamares ware
Kantzios, Niki Holmes, *64*, 67, 94
Kapitanakos (chair of special shoreline committee), 106
Karetsou, Alexandra (Ephor of Antiquities of the Herakleion province), 70
Kato Zakros, 55, 92, 97, 102, 103
palace of, 119
Kenchreai (harbor for Corinth), 101, 102, 103, 105
Knossos
as administrative center, 74
harbors of, *54*, 55
overseas trade and, 118
palace of, 119
"Palace Style" or LM II wares from, 126, 127
Phoenician finds, 140
tablets from, 76
Unexplored Mansion and LM II wares, 127
Koeffel and Esser Company, 97
Koehl, Robert, 139
Kokkinos Pyrgos, 72
Kommos. *See also* excavation at Kommos
abandonment of, 23, 39

aerial views of, *15, 16*
as archaeological park, 10, 70, 71
chronology of, 11–13
as "da-wo," 76
development restrictions around the site, 68
digital publishing of Kommos volumes, 148–49
digital source (T-space), 149
domestic economy of, 96, 128–31
erosion by waves, 55–56
extent of LM structures, 23
fencing in the site, 69
Greek remains at, 78
as harbor of Hagia Triada, 76
as harbor of Mesara, 35
as a harbor site, 55
negotiations for site expropriation, 105–7
plan of Building P, *37*
plan of Building T, *32*
plan of hillside houses, *21*
plan of hilltop houses, *20*
prehistoric settlement of, 73–76, 128
1976 property expropriation and purchase, 12, 105–7
1978 property purchase, 88
1990 property transfer and extension of site, 68–70, 121
publishing program for *Kommos* volumes, 147–49
renewal of houses in, 74, 75
revival of overseas trade, 75, 118
as rural shrine, 77
settlement of, 16, 18
site preservation, 23, 142
site reports, 13
topographical plan, *19*
topographical plans for, 105–6
views and visions of site, 141–43
website, 149
Kommos V, 13, 80, 98
Kotsifakis, Michaelis (mayor of Pitsidia), 70–71
Kyprakis, Manolis, 65
Kyprakis, Petros, 108

lamps, Roman, 45, *46*, 132
La Rosa, Enzo, 117
La Rosa, Vincenzo, 79
laurel wreath (bronze) with ivory berries, 49, *50*
Lechaion (near Corinth), 53
Lendas (Lebena), 53, 72, 77

Lethaios (modern Geropotamos) River, 72
Leto, 50, 140
Levi, Doro, 106, 108
lily fresco (House X), *28, 29*, 74, 93–94
limpet shells, 130–31
Linear A clay tablets, 76
Lissos, Temple of Asklepios, 136, *137*, 138
"LM Man," 67
loomweights, 35, 56, *56*, 138

Malia, palace of, 55, 92, 119
Manisoudakis, George (front loader driver), 86–87, 91
Marinatos, Spyridon, 106, 136
Markou, Mary, 9
Martin, Paul, 100
Matala
    in 1972, *52*
    Greco-Roman shipshed in, 53
    Greek remains at, 78
    as harbor, 53, 72, 77, 104
    road to, 62, 63
    as tourist center, 65, 70
McDonald, William, 96
McEnroe, John, *22*, 86, 108, 120
    and Temple B, *42*
McKenzie, Duncan, 144
Melanouri, 63
Menelaos, shipwreck of, 59
Mesara Message, The, 67
Mesara Plain, 72–73. *See also* western Mesara
metalworking, 34, 129
Millet, Nick, 139
Minnesota Messenia Expedition, 96, 104
Mires, 62, 67, 68, 72
Mitten, David, 100
Mochlos, *54*, 55
Monuments of Minos: Rethinking the Minoan Palace (2002), 119
mortars, 128

Nefertum, faience figurine, 43, 139
net mender, bronze, 56
New York Times, The, 89
Nisos Peninsula, 59
Nixon, Gordon, 94
Nixon, Lucia, 92
North American Cretan studies, 145–45
North House, 23–24
    plan of, *22*

North Stoa, 33–34. *See also* Building T
    discovery of, 13, 120–21, *122, 123*
    evidence of reuse, 35
    grain-grinding bins in, 34
    painted plasters, 94
    restored view of, *32*
nymphs, 49

Oblique House, 24
olive oil, 129
Oren, Eliezer, 116
Orientalization, 139
Orr, Douglas, *42*, 88, 120
orthostate façades, 30, *31*, 33, 38
Ostia, 103

Palace of Minos at Knossos, The (Evans), 103, 144
palaces, characteristics of Minoan, 73, 74
Palace Style (LM II). *See* pottery
Pandeleimon, Saint. *See* Hagios Pandeleimon
Pan (god of flocks and groves), fragmentary limestone relief of, *49*, 132–33
Papadoplaka ("the priest's slab") reef, 55, 57, 66
Papandreiou, Andreas, 121
Papayiannakis, Aristotle, 121
patitiri. *See* press beds
Paximadhia Islands, 130, 142
Pediada pottery, 117
Peschke, George V., 101
Petras, palace of, 119
Petrokephali, 62
Phaistos, 62, 145
    destruction of, 74
    Greek acropolis at, 78
    Minoan palace of, *73*
    as "pa-i-to," 76
    palace of, 119
    prehistoric settlement of, 73, 74
    rebuilding of, 79
    revival of (ca. 1150 B.C.), 75
Phoenician Pottery of Cyprus, The (Bikai, 1987), 116
Phoenicians, Tripillar Shrine and pottery of, 43, 90, 116, 139, 140
pig remains, 131
Pisidia (Turkey), 63
pithoi, 22, 37
    Cypriot, *58*
    on the hilltop, 18, 24

Pitsidia, 10
- in 1978, *61*
- accommodation in, 108
- excavation headquarters at, 65–66
- excavation storage area, *64, 65*
- Giuliana Bianco's sketches of town life, *66, 67, 69, 70*
- a house in, *70*
- layout of town, 63
- mayor's "public road," *69, 70*
- musicians in, *67*
- road to, *62*
- town square, *66*

plasters, painted, 94
Platon, Nikolas (Ephor of Boeotia), 101–2, 136
Polaroid Corporation, 97
Pomerance, Leon, 97
Poseidon
- cylindrical altar to, 49–50, 133
- sanctuary at Isthmia, 101, 102

pot stands, 24, 29
potter's wheel, 24
pottery
- bridge-spouted vessels, 18, *23*
- from Building N, 37
- ceramic chronology, 62, 80–81, 138
- fabrics, 115
- House with the Snake Tube and LM II wares, 126–27
- from House X, 29, *39, 58*
- Knossian wares, 115
- LM II or "Palace Style," 75, 126–27
- LM II vessel types, *127*
- and Minoan chronology, 62
- from North House, 23
- from post MM II hilltop rooms, 18
- prevalence as artifacts, 115
- from Temple C, 49
- "The Strange and Wonderful" box, 115, 116

pottery kiln (LM IA), 122, *123*
press beds (olive/wine), 24, *25*, 129
Princeton University Press, 147
Prinias, Temple at, 138
Progress into the Past (McDonald), 96

querns, 128

Ras Shamra (Ugarit), 95
Reese, David, 130
resins, 117

rhyta
- bull's head, 18, *21*
- LM funnel-shaped, 24, *25*, 110
- polychrome conical, 18, *22*

Rinaldo, John, 100
rituals or religious activities, 18, 141
- Building AA and, 30
- Cretan adoption of foreign deities, 50, 139, 140
- cult statues and, 47
- deities worshipped, 49–50, 132, 139–40
- House X shrine, 29
- lustration or bathing, 29, 45, 49
- meals and sacrifices and the Greek Sanctuary, 45, 57, 128, 131, 133, 138, 141, 142
- offerings and Temple C, 49, 131, 133
- offerings and the Tripillar Shrine, *42, 43, 44*, 90, 139–40
- rhyta and, 18, 24
- snake tubes and, 27
- in Temple A, 41
- trinities of deities, 50, 139, 140
- votive use of marble anchor stock, 57
- worship of groups of tapering pillars, 43, 50

roads
- east-west Road 17, 29, 30, *33*, 74, 103–4
- on the hillside, 27
- on the hilltop, 23, 24

Robinson, Charles Alexander, Jr., 100
Royal Ontario Museum (ROM), 97, 98, 139
Rutter, Jeremy, 39
- on imported wares, 117, 118

Rutter, Nick, 67

Sabourin, Josée, 122
Sardinia
- bronze scrap from, 116
- collar-necked jar from, *58*
- pottery from, 37, 57, 75, 80, 94, 116

scarabs, 43
SCM Corporation, 97
Scranton, Robert, 101, 102, 105
seal, bird on steatite bead, *29*
sea levels, changes in, 56
Sedra, Adel (Provost, University of Toronto), 98
Sekhmet (Egyptian goddess of war), faience figurine, 43, *44*, 89, 139, 140
Shaw, Alexander, 10, 67, 102
- and orthostate façade, *31*

INDEX 169

Shaw, Joseph W., 12
    on Arthur Evans's work, 144
    aims for excavations at Kommos, 92, 96, 115, 128
    on an archaeologist's obligation to publish, 146
    archaeological survey walks, 104, 134–35
    on contributors to Kommos volumes, 147–48
    discovery of prayer to Artemis, 135
    early visits to Pitsidia and Kommos, 65, 104
    educational and professional background, 100–4
    and land mines at Kommos, 86
    made honorary citizen of Pitsidia, 70
    on writing preliminary reports, 145–46
Shaw, Maria C., 10
    and bronze horse figurine, *90*
    on Building P as shipsheds, 39, 79–80, 124–25
    discovery of lily fresco in House X, 93–94
    educational background, 102
    made honorary citizen of Pitsidia, 70
    and orthostate façade, *31*
    in Pitsidia storeroom, *64*
    and press bed, *25*
Shaw, Robin, 10, 67, 102
sheep/goat remains, 128, 131
shield, bronze, *42, 43*, 140
shipsheds, 39, 79–80, 124–25, 143
shipwrecks, Minoan, 59
Sidon, 103
Siva, 63
slabs, stone
    as bases for vessels, 18, 129
    as press beds, 129
    for ritual bathing or lustration, 29, 45, 49
    as washing platform, 24
slab stands, 130–31
snake tube vessel (LM III), *26, 27*, 110–11
Social Sciences and Humanities Research Council (SSHRC), 9, 97
Sotios Secundus, 135
South Stoa, 35, *36*
    discovery of, 13, 70, 122–23
spearhead, 140
Sphakakis, Papageorghis (priest), 108, *110*
Spinthakis, Fofo, 108
Spinthakis, Nikos, *109*, 111
Spyridakis, Zacharias, 65, 105
Staedtler Mars Company, 97
stairways, 33, 35, 146

in Building B of Greek Sanctuary, 47, *48*
stamnostatis (stone slab base), 129, *130*
statue bases, 45, 47, 132, 136, 138
Stone, Louise, 97
storerooms
    in Building P, 38, 124, 125
    in Building T, 34, 35
    on hilltop, 18, 24
"Strange and Wonderful" box, 115, 116
Stratis, James, 71
Strom, Cy, 147
Stroud, Ronald, 100

Temple A, 11, 41
    discovery of, 12
    dump for, 120
Temple B, 11, 41, *42, 43*, 47, 139, 141. *See also* Tripillar Shrine
    discovery of, 12
    dump for, 120
    limpet shells and, 130
    restored geometric plan of, *42*
    slab stands and, *131*
Temple C, 11, 41, *42*, 45, 47, 120, 142
    Altar C, 12, 47, *48, 137*, 138
    Altar H, 45, 47, *136*
    altars and offerings, 131, 133
    changes to, 43
    cult statue(s) and, 47, 49, 132, 136
    deities worshipped at, 50, 132–33
    discovery of, 12, 111, 132–33
    fire damage to, 49
    marble anchor stock, 57
    pig bones from, 131
    plan of, 136, *137*, 138
    restored plan of, *46*, 47
    statue base, 45, 47, 132, 136
terracotta
    bull figurine, 47, *48*, 87–88
    horses, 140
Thebes, 101
threshold blocks, 23, 24
    reuse of, 37
timbers, use of, 38
Times (London), 103
trade, overseas, 18. *See also* imported wares
    and anchors, 94–95
    and Building T, 35
    ceramic evidence for, 57, 80, 94, 118
    and Phoenicians, 43

170 KOMMOS: A MINOAN HARBOR TOWN

post-Roman access to Crete, 72
pottery and, 57
revival and Building P, 75, 118
routes and means of, 117
and short-necked amphoras, 39
Travlos, John, 101
trenchmasters, selection criteria for, 66, 146
trinities of deities, 50, 139, 140
Tripillar Shrine, 41, *42*, 43, 139–40. *See also* Temple B
    base and pillar tenon for, *42*
    discovery of, 12, 89–90
    offerings and, *42*, 43, *44*, 90
    and the Phoenicians, 43, 139, 140, 141
    pillars as aniconic deities, 50
    plans and elevations of, *42*
tripod base, 49
Tritsis, Antonis, 101
Tsoutsouros, 72
T-space (digital source for Kommos), 149
tuna remains, 130
Tushingham, Douglas, 97
Tymbaki, 72
Tyre, 103

Ugarit (Ras Shamra), 95
Uluburun shipwreck, 59
unguentaria (containers for oil or perfume), 49
University Museum of the University of Pennsylvania, 145
University of Toronto, 9, 97, 98

Van de Moortel, Aleydis, 80, 122
Vanderpool, Gene, 100–1
Van der Rohe, Ludwig Mies, 101
vase, incised black glazed, 43, 140
Vigles, 18
Vlassakis, Evangelis, 122
Volakas, 57

walkway (MM II), 30, 34
Wardell, Timothy, 9
warden ("neokoros"), 47
Warren, Peter, 103
Watkinson, Charles, 9
Watrous, L. Vance, 80, 111, 147
    identification of imported wares, 116, 117
    on short-necked amphoras, 39
Western Anatolian vessels, 117

western Mesara
    archaeological landscapes in, 62
    ceramic sequences in, 80–81
    coastline and harbor potential, 51, 53
    dimensions of, 72
    map of, *51*
    prehistoric settlement of, 73
Wickerson, Lorne, 9
Wiener, Malcolm, 97, 145
wines, 43, *45*, 57, 117
Winter, Frederick, 97
Wiseman, James, 100
Workman, John, 100
World War II, 84, 86
Wright, James, 89

Young, Rodney, 136

Zakros. *See* Kato Zakros
Zeus, inscription to, 49–50, 133